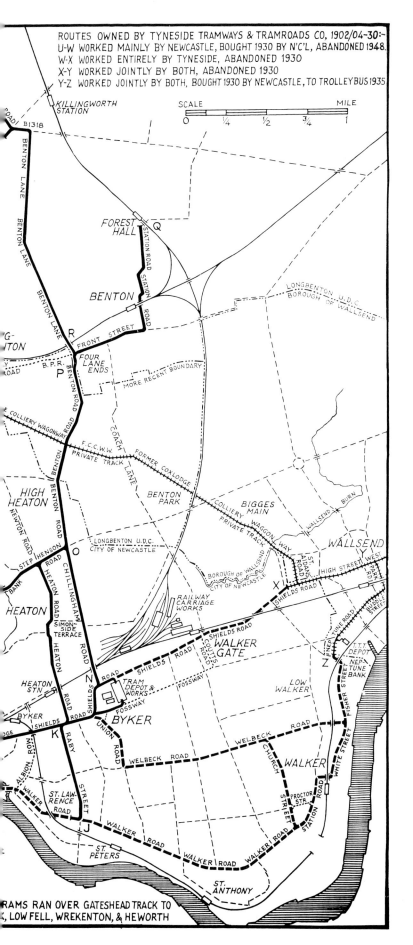

ROUTES OWNED BY TYNESIDE TRAMWAYS & TRAMROADS CO, 1902/04-30:-
U-W WORKED MAINLY BY NEWCASTLE, BOUGHT 1930 BY N'C'L, ABANDONED 1948.
W-X WORKED ENTIRELY BY TYNESIDE, ABANDONED 1930
X-Y WORKED JOINTLY BY BOTH, ABANDONED 1930
Y-Z WORKED JOINTLY BY BOTH, BOUGHT 1930 BY NEWCASTLE, TO TROLLEYBUS 1935

SCALE
0   ¼   ½   ¾   MILE
1

...RAMS RAN OVER GATESHEAD TRACK TO
..., LOW FELL, WREKENTON, & HEWORTH

CHRISTOPHER R. IRWIN

Silver Link Publishing Ltd

The Coach House,
Garstang Road, St Michael's,
Lancashire, PR3 OTG.

CONTENTS

AUTHOR'S ACKNOWLEDGEMENTS

A great many people have helped in the preparation of this book, not least the residents of the four towns concerned, who have given freely of their time and memories.

In particular I should like to thank: Mr G. Baddeley for photographs, the North of England Open Air Museum and Mr J. Lawson for access to archives and for printing; Mr R.R. Clark for the use of his photographs; John Fozard for providing and printing photographs (mainly from the Bob Mack Collection); Gateshead, South Shields & Sunderland libraries for information; Mr J.C. Gillham for the superb maps drawn specially for this book; Nigel and Jayne Harris of SLP for their help and tolerance; Mr G. Hearse for photographs and permission to use material from his books, Mr S.G. Jackman for photographs; Mr E. Keogh for information; Mr C. Meddes for help with printing and for information; Mr J. Meredith for photographs and printing; the National Tramway Museum and Mr G. Wilton for supplying and printing photographs (mainly from the Norman Forbes Collection); Newcastle City Engineer's Department for copying the Library photographs; Newcastle Libraries for photographs and information; Mr M. O'Connor and Mr J. Price for information; Mr H.B. Priestley for photographs; Mr T. Steele for photographs and information; Mr T. Stephenson for colour photographs, and Mr T. Wickens for photographs. Finally, I would like to thank my wife Mary, to whom this book is dedicated; also the staff of The Book House, Ravenstonedale, for their toleration of the chaos caused during the preparation of this work.

Every effort has been made to trace the source of photographs used. If any are wrongly attributed I apologise and would welcome correct information.

FRONT COVER: On a sunny day in May 1953, Sunderland car No. 33 is seen on the seafront at Seaburn. Like all Sunderland cars, it carried a pantograph, rather than a pole, for current collection, giving it a rather odd appearance to British eyes. No 33 was one of the eight cars bought from Huddersfield Corporation in 1938, when it was only seven years old. With their flat ends and generally modern appearance, these cars were quite distinctive both in Huddersfield and Sunderland. They were built by the English Electric Company; it is a great pity none were preserved. *I.R. Davidson.*

LEFT: The final extension of the Durham Road route, in Sunderland, in February 1949 was the last significant piece of tramway construction in Britain for more than 40 years. This fine view shows the sweep across the valley, with the intermediate terminus at Grindon Lane visible beyond the lorry. On the right are a group of post-war 'pre-fabs,' which although designed as a short-term measure lasted for many years – indeed, in some towns, examples survive in the 1990s! *John Fozard Collection.*

*Copyright © May 1990,
Christopher R. Irwin/Silver Link
Publishing Ltd.*

*Designed by Barbara Allen,
Leading Edge Press & Publishing.*

Jacket design by Nigel Harris.

First published in the United Kingdom, May 1990.

Imagesetting by Ps&QS, Liverpool and printed in the United Kingdom by The Amadeus Press, Huddersfield, Yorkshire.

ISBN: 0 947971 45 9

> ***PLEASE NOTE:**
> A CIP record for this book
> is available from the British Library.*

THE NATIONAL TRAMWAY MUSEUM

Tramcar preservation in this country started in 1948, when a group of enthusiasts bought a little open-top tram from Southampton. Built in 1903, it had survived millions of miles of daily running, to say nothing of two world wars, and they could not bear the thought of it being broken up for scrap.

This was some three years before the first railway preservation scheme (the Talyllyn Railway) and nobody had any clear ideas on how to preserve a vehicle than ran on rails. Other trams were rescued from the scrapman, and although storage was arranged for some cars whilst others went on display at Beaulieu and Clapham museums, several were lost to vandals and the weather. The Tramway Museum Society was formed in 1955 and in 1959 a disused quarry was found at Crich, in Derbyshire, which would form a suitable site for a museum.

This was only just in time, for in the next few years the closures at Leeds, Sheffield and Glasgow, unleashed a flood of trams. These were to form the basis of the Museum's fleet. From the beginning, the first priority of the Society was to house the cars under cover, which meant that a running track had to wait, but in 1963 services started, appropriately enough with a horse-tram. Electric operation followed in 1964. Today, one mile of track gives a reasonable length of ride yet also affords the visitor the chance to sample several different vehicles.

About 50 trams are owned by the Society, although some are stored away from the site. Each year about fifteen cars are brought into operating condition for the summer, with the aim of providing as much variety as possible. There is an exhibition of tramway history in one of the depots, while the others are opened daily to allow visitors to see vehicles not in service that day. In 1990, a new Exhibition Hall is being fitted out which should vastly improve facilities to view the the trams.

In recent years the importance of the enterprise has been recognised through its new title, the National Tramway Museum. It is run by volunteers, with the aid of a few dedicated full-time staff, and is dependent on entrance fees and other sales ventures for raising the money required in the preservation and operation of historic tramcars. This can be considerable - the restoration work on a car can cost arounf £60,000 – more than 100 times its original cost!

The Museum is open during Easter week and every weekend until the end of October. From mid-May to the end of September it is also open Monday to Thursday, with Friday opening during the school holidays. Admission is £3.00 for adults, with reductions for senior citizens, children, & large parties. This includes admission to all parts of the Museum and unlimited tram rides. There are special events, such as the Leeds Transport Day, on many weekends. The latest details of times and events may be obtained by telephoning 0773-852565.

Chris Irwin,
Ravenstonedale,
Cumbria, April 1990.

SELECT BIBLIOGRAPHY:

The following books are by no means all that touch on the topic of north-eastern urban transport, but together they cover most of the tramway and trolleybus developments in the area. Regrettably, most are out of print but can normally be obtained through libraries or the search service provided by most second-hand bookshops.

Abell, P.H: *British Tramway Guide.* (Author, 1975).
Burrows, G: *The Trolleybuses of South Shields.* (Trolleybooks, 1976).
Canneaux, T.P & Hanson, N.H: *The Trolleybuses of Newcastle upon Tyne.* (Trolleybooks, 1975).
Hearse, G.S: *Remember the Trams: Newcastle.* (Author, 1978).
Hearse, G.S: *The Tramways of Gateshead.* (Author, 1965).
Hearse, G.S: *The Tramways of Jarrow & South Shields.* (Author, 1971).
Hearse, G.S: *The Tramways of Northumberland.* (Author, 1961).
Joyce, J: *Roads and Rails of Tyne & Wear, 1900-1980.* (Ian Allan, 1975).
Staddon, S.A: *The Tramways of Sunderland.* (Advertiser Press, 1964).

═══ INTRODUCTION ═══

DURING the last half of the nineteenth and the first half of the twentieth centuries, the banks of the rivers Tyne and Wear in the North-East of England were to become one of the greatest engineering centres of the world. Under the guidance of a remarkable group of industrial entrepreneurs the region's workshops and shipyards poured out a continual stream of manufactures which were exported to every corner of the globe to meet the enormous demands created by the expansion of both the British Empire and the underdeveloped regions of the Americas, both North and South.

This expansion, added to the existing coal production of the area, led to the creation of what would now be known as a conurbation encompassing both banks of the Tyne, with a similar but smaller effect on Wearside a few miles to the south. From Scotswood in the west, factories and houses formed a continuous belt joining the various small fishing communities and river wharves to Tynemouth and South Shields at the mouth of the river. On the Wear, the ancient villages of Monkwearmouth, to the

During the bitter winter of 1947, passengers hurry for the shelter of No. 183, outside Newcastle Central Station. At such times the usually despised trams came into their own, for they could keep running long after other transport was snowbound: indeed, in Sheffield they actually towed buses up icy hills! There was nothing like the inside of a tram in bad weather - the distinctive smell of wet clothes and wet people, clouds of pipe and cigarette smoke, steamed-up windows, and above all, the feeling that you were safe inside and that the tram would get you home. *Newcastle Libraries.*

north, and Bishopwearmouth became the Borough of Sunderland, the town that led the world in shipbuilding.

In many other places this would have resulted in one 'super-city' and the loss of identity of the various communities, but the people of Northumberland and Durham have always been rugged individualists. Even the relatively recent creation of the county of Tyne and Wear has not altered the determination of Wearsiders that they are not as the people of Tynemouth, nor has it allowed Newcastle to swallow up Gateshead next door as Manchester, for instance, has done with Salford. As with the

communities, so it was with transport and the region had a diversity of horse, steam and later, electric, tramways unmatched anywhere else in Great Britain.

This book is concerned with those tramways and in particular with the period after the last World War, from 1945 until the final closure at Sunderland in 1954. It is not intended to be a history of those tramways as that task has already been undertaken in an admirable fashion by two local authors, George Hearse and the late S.A. Staddon. In their books the reader will be able to find the specialised details of motors and controllers, tickets and fare stages, and all the minutiae so beloved of the enthusiast. I hope to capture some of my own enthusiasm for the tramcar in its setting, whether gliding through the stately streets of Newcastle at night, lights ablaze and gong sounding, or creeping furtively on single track down cobbled back-alleys to reach obscure works and harbours known only to those who laboured there.

The choice of 1945 is not accidental. During the last war, in many ways, time came to a halt, and schemes for abandoning the trams, as in Newcastle or extending the systems, as in Sunderland, were tidied away to the top shelf in the office 'for the duration'. With reduced labour forces, a minimum of spare parts, and carrying a load of passengers never dreamed of by their designers, the tramways took the munitions workers, the dockers, the schoolchildren, and the housewives, backwards and forwards day by day with a regularity which ensured that few even noticed their existence. When the struggle was over and Europe was at peace again, the humble tramcar found it was no longer wanted and in spite of the warnings of the few who were rather more forseeing than most of us, in a few years public and councils alike, beguiled by the shiny new motorbuses, had condemned their old friend to oblivion. The sceptics were right, of course, and in due time the tramcar was to return in the shape of the Metro, in a nice bright yellow livery and pretending to be an electric train. But that is another story!

Fortunately, there were a few people who were not prepared to let the tramcar disappear without making

Left: Where it all began. From the earliest days of wheeled vehicles people have tried to provide a smooth track by laying wood or stone. Early in the last century, blocks were laid in city streets, especially on hills, and examples were to be found in most industrial towns. Needing very little maintainance, many lasted until the 1950s, when the decline in horse-drawn traffic prompted their removal. Fortunately, two good examples survive in Newcastle, this one in Hanover Street and an interesting 'dual gauge' version in Delaval Road. From these stone tramways it was a short step to adding the guiding qualities of the flanged wheel, resulting in the street tramway as depicted in this book. Incidentally, the word 'tram' comes from the old Scandanavian word for a baulk or block of wood. *Newcastle City Engineer.*

Below: A neat bit of overhead - but where's the track? Fourteen years after the last Newcastle tram ran, this silent reminder remained in Pilgrim Street. Trolleybuses still had two years of life before they followed the trams into oblivion, ousted by the all-conquering, albeit smelly and noisy, diesel bus. But this short stretch of tram wire remained. At the foot of the pole on the left is a 'section box', where the underground electricity supply cables emerged and were connected to the overhead wire by the cables curved above the street. In turn these tram wires connected with those for the trolleybuses, out of sight behind the photographer. It was cheaper to leave these few yards in the air than install a new section box. *Newcastle City Engineer.*

Left, upper: The lower deck of an unidentified Class 'B' car. There were 75 examples, five built just after the First World War, with the remaining 70 in the 1920s. They were all broadly similar, having Peckham P22 trucks with air brakes, and seating 36 people downstairs with 26 upstairs. Over the years a few were modified, one even appearing for a short time as a six-wheel car with a bogie at one end only! The straight staircases were unusual; they helped speed loading and unloading but, as can be seen, they did steal useful seating space. Trams were fairly narrow and the longitudinal seating gave plenty of room for standing passengers. By 1948, they were obsolete and it is small wonder that passengers regarded the new trolleybuses as a marked improvement. *Newcastle Libraries.*

Left, lower: A typical crew pose at Scotswood Bridge turning circle - the bridge itself can be seen reflected in the car windows. Uniforms were provided by the Corporation and the old tunics (which buttoned up to the neck) had not long been abandoned when this picture was taken. The conductress is carrying the tools of her trade; a bag for change, whistle dangling from her lapel, and a 'Bell' ticket punch. This last device not only made the holes which indicated to which stage the ticket was valid, but retained the little circle of paper. Thus if there was any discrepancy in the money paid-in at the end of the day, the various little bits of coloured paper could be counted, a somewhat tedious process! Her ticket rack will be in the bag; normally it was held in the left hand and tickets issued and clipped in one sweeping movement with the right. *A.D. Packer Collection.*

Above: The Last Car up Westgate. This was A comic post-card by F. Macleod, hopefully not taken from life! The original card was had crudely printed colouring and was sold in many towns with tramways, the wording being personalised by using a local destination. *North of England Open Air Museum, Beamish.*

some sort of record of its passing. Years before, when trams first came to the North-East they were a source of great pride and for every tramway there is a multitude of official photographs laying the track, erecting the overhead, testing the cars, and finally, of course, the Mayor in all his ceremonial glory driving the first tram (and usually getting his chain of office entangled with the controller handle). But after the war the task was left to those few enthusiasts who loved the tramcar and its habits, the men who had tried and failed in many cases to plead for its future and modernisation. It was a hard task, because film was almost impossible to obtain, travel was difficult, and many of them were still in obscure places at home and abroad in the service of their country. But they made their record, and although in many cases the cameras and film available to them were not of good quality, their pictures have captured for us the essence of the tramway scene.

A word or two about the book's approach. For each town I have included a short history and a map to help those unfamiliar with the area. Then, after a brief look around the town centre we visit routes in turn, travelling in a clockwise direction. Hopefully I have included at least one scene that has some memories for those who live in the area. One thing missing which one might expect are

pictures of trams among the factories around Newcastle. Those who knew what was made in many of those factories, and remember 'Dora', will know why. And some of the pictures have been published before. For their re-use you must blame me. I like them!

Today, 40 or so years after the trams retired, the old Dunston Staithes and the Gasworks at Gateshead are revitalised as the National Garden Festival. The site is in two parts and to take visitors from one section to the other, it has a tramway. On this are running some of the trams seen in these pages, saved from the scrapman's depredations by the dedication (or eccentricity) of a group of enthusiasts. By its very nature it is a clean, aseptic affair with the trams beautifully restored and running in an environment considerably different from that of their working life. This book, I hope, will serve as a reminder of a means of transport and a way of life totally different from that of today.

Chris Irwin,
Ravenstonedale,
Cumbria,
April 1990

Chapter 1
NEWCASTLE

NEWCASTLE is the principal city of the North East of England and is situated on the North bank of the River Tyne, which separates the historic counties of Durham and Northumberland. The Romans had a fort here, but the development of the present City really began with the building of the 'New Castle' in AD1080 as part of the Normans' campaign to subjugate the North. The town had a fairly stormy history, including more than one occupation by the Scots, but in the more settled times of the late 18th Century it began to flourish as a regional centre. Most of the City as we see it today is the result of the inspired alliance of three men, Richard Grainger the builder and developer, John Dobson the architect, and John Clayton, the Town Clerk. Mainly during the years 1835-40 these three laid out and built a commercial town centre which has no equal in England.

As industry developed along the river the housing needed for the workers had to be built beside and behind the City, swallowing many of the existing mining communities, such as Gosforth. Much of the earliest housing near the river had deteriorated so much that it was cleared between the wars and vast new estates built well away from the centre, such as those around Benton. This en-

(continued on page 12)

Neville Street - one of the best public transport interchanges anywhere in the United Kingdom. John Dobson's magnificent Central Station on the left was served not only by most East Coast Main Line trains, but was also the focal point for a network of steam and electric lines serving Northumberland, Durham, Carlisle, and the Borders. Outside, a four-track tramway accommodated (at its peak) some 13 all-day and three rush-hour services, including some through services from Gateshead. In the background can be seen St. Mary's Cathedral and on the right is the imposing bulk of the County Hotel. Alongside the hotel is Grainger Street with its double junctions allowing trams to turn either East or West into Neville Street. *Newcastle Libraries.*

Right: The conductor of No. 107 seemingly keeps his tram firmly on the leash as they proceed down Neville Street. Keeping hold of the rope is a sensible precaution when propelling the trolley pole in case the trolley de-wires. The figure on the top deck is the second conductor, needed aboard these enormous Class 'F' cars to deal with the high number of passengers they could carry – more than 100 including standees. Originally, No.107 was similar to preserved car No. 102, but was rebuilt during the First World War with vestibules and an extended top deck. Possibly because of a lack of materials, the car was fitted with a straight steel staircase at one end and wooden stairs at the other - a curiosity it retained all its life. *S.G. Jackman.*

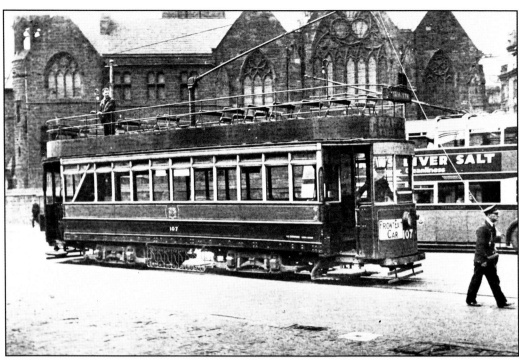

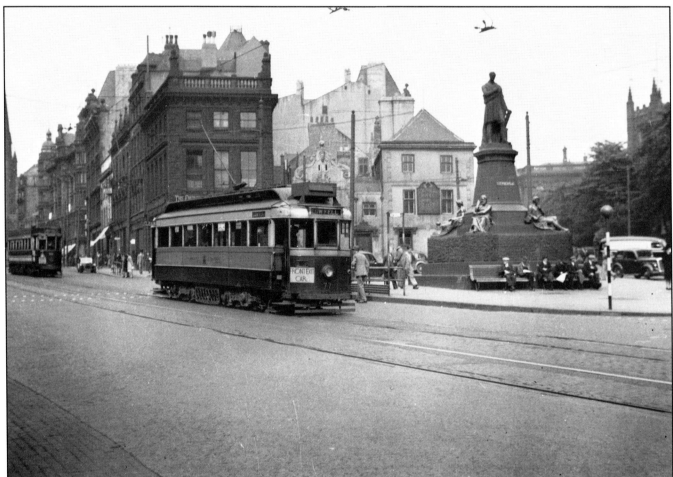

On a rather grey day, probably in 1947, No. 77 (bound for Low Fell) loads passengers under the watchful eye of George Stephenson. This monument to Tyneside's most famous engineer was designed by a local man, W.G. Lough. The original design included ornamental railings round the base, but these have long since disappeared. The four figures reclining rather uncomfortably on the plinth represent an engineer, a miner, a navvy, and a smith. The whole edifice cost around £5,000 and was unveiled on October 2 1862. The buildings behind the tram have now been replaced by a modern office block. *R.R. Clark.*

As the conductor of No.193 swings the trolley pole, a Fenham bound trolleybus slips round the corner of the *County Hotel* from Grainger Street. The impressive spire in the background belongs to St. Mary's Cathedral and was designed by Joseph Hansom, of 'Hansom Cab' fame. It graces the 1844 Pugin church building which became the Roman Catholic Cathedral in 1860 when the first Bishop was appointed. The cost of £2,625 seems modest today, but it had taken the congregation 16 years to pay off the debt on the original building and it was not until 1872 that they were able to afford the spire. In the foreground we can see the Spital and North Eastern Hotels but regrettably this fine frontage has been replaced by a modern office block. *(R.R. Clark)*

Above: This view was taken during the last days of trams in Newcastle, with the Corporation trams all gone and the last Gateshead cars confined to the few hundred yards of track between the river and Central Station. The double line of studs in the road marks a pedestrian crossing - its orange globe can be seen on the right. These were known as 'Belisha Beacons' after Sir Leslie Hore-Belisha, the 1930s Minister of Transport who introduced them. The single-deck trams, Nos. 8 and 16, date from the 1920s, but the double-deck No. 27 is now 50 years old. *R.R. Clark.*

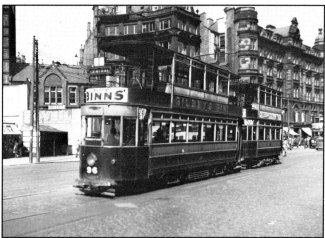

Above: Another view in Neville Street, showing part of the four-track layout here. Tram No. 96 (foreground) was one of the three 'F' class cars rebuilt in their early years. Originally like No. 102, they acquired top deck covers, extended upper decks, and lengthened platforms. The driver's vestibules were added, in 1938. There were seats for 92 passengers and they could officially carry 147, but George Hearse comments that sometimes there were more than 200 on board! In their rebuilt guise they were claimed to be the largest tramcars ever to run in England. *R.R. Clark.*

couraged the development of a dense network of tramways with some quite lengthy lines. In due course, too, it was to encourage the development of electric railways and, later, the Metro.

Newcastle's first trams appeared in 1878, when the Corporation built a small network of horse tramways and leased them to a private company, the Newcastle & Gosforth Tramways & Carriage Company. Although steam engines were tried in 1879 they were not a success and the horse trams continued until just after the expiry of the lease. As the company and the Corporation could not agree, trams then ceased altogether, but electrification work was already well under way and 8 months later, on December 16 1901, the Corporation's first electric car .made its way through the town.

Like the horse-drawn tramways, the electric lines were of standard gauge. Power was supplied by a generating station at Manors, which still exists as an empty shell used for parking 'Busways' service vehicles. The Transport Offices at one end of the building have a fine coloured glass window over the entrance showing both horse and electric trams. Power was also supplied to other municipal enterprises and for street lighting, while the surplus was sold. It was closed in 1936. The construction gangs pressed ahead with great vigour and by 1904 the basic network along the main roads was complete.

As the tram lines were built to the west and north they met those of the Tyneside Tramways & Tramroads Company, which linked Wallsend and North Shields, and also had a cross-country branch as long as the main line which went first to Gosforth, then up the Great North Road to Gosforth Park. After the inevitable arguments, agreement was reached whereby Tyneside cars could run into the City and Newcastle cars could use the Gosforth Park line, a section which was taken over by the City when the Tyneside trams finished. Over the years, extensions continued to be made as the trams followed (or in some cases preceded) the development of housing. At maximum there were over 50 route miles, not including joint services. The first link with Gateshead came in 1923, across the High Level Bridge, to be followed in 1928 by the New Tyne Bridge. After this, the three main North-South routes were jointly worked, and even the purely Gateshead services (with minor exceptions) ran into the City. Up to this time the tramway policy had been steadily expansionist and although buses (under the name Blue Bus Services) were operated they were mainly long routes to places well outside the City. There had been a couple of route closures but they were of lines which had been rather speculative in nature and on which traffic was never likely to develop.

In the 1930s, policy changed rapidly and trolley-buses were proposed in 1931 and actually introduced in 1935, taking over the long East-West route along Walker Road and Westgate Road. It was clear that the tramways had only a few years to go and if it had not been for the war they would probably all have been closed by the early 1940s. As it was, they had a few years reprieve but as new vehicles once again became available tram-scrapping recommenced and by the end of 1949 all purely Newcastle services had gone except for a few rush hour extras from Elswick Works to Byker. On March 4, the last trams participating in the joint routes were replaced by buses. Yet for over a year it continued to play host to Gateshead trams, although they were only allowed as far as Central Station, but they too were living on borrowed time and on August 4 1951 the last Tyneside tram of all rolled into Gateshead's Sunderland Road Depot.

Above: This is what the traveller would have seen as he emerged from the East end of the Central Station Portico in 1950. Gateshead car No. 27 is waiting for a single-deck car to clear the crossover before reversing. In the distance another single-deck car departs for Gateshead. Hidden from sight behind the trams is the Stephenson Monument. The buildings behind the monument have been replaced by an astonishingly ugly office block which projects half-way across the street, but the tall buildings in the distance remain. The block to the left of the single-deck car houses both Barclay's Bank and Lloyd's Register of Shipping, a reminder of Newcastle's importance as a port. *R.R. Clark.*

Above: Reversing outside Central Station we see No. 120, the last survivor of the Class 'A' trams, later re-numbered 24. Behind it is a somewhat striking group of buildings now replaced by a modern office block. It is clear that the architects of the three buildings had different ideas on how to make their edifices imposing, yet they blend together remarkably well. On the right were the offices of Employers' Liability Assurance Corporation and the Clerical, Medical & General Life Assurance Society. Station Chambers at No 10 had many tenants including the Neville Estate Company, whose name can be seen in the windows above Phillips. *R.R. Clark.*

Nos. 120 and 267 are at the loading island outside the County Hotel in 1947, while a Vauxhall passes at a speed which not only blurs the shot but attracts the attention of a passer-by. Over the road can be seen another form of electric traction, a battery-powered van (Bird's Laundries). This was one of the biggest of Newcastle's 13 laundry concerns, with its headquarters in Claremont Road and three other 'receiving offices' around the city. Battery vehicles are made today on the Team Valley Trading Estate and will no doubt become ever more popular as concern grows over vehicle pollution. Both the *County Hotel* and its brasher next door neighbour, the *Victoria and Comet*, still serve the hungry traveller - the latter as Yate's Wine Lodge. *R.R. Clark.*

NEWCASTLE'S TRAM FLEET

At the end of the last war Newcastle Corporation operated seven classes of passenger trams, but many were withdrawn very quickly when scrapping re-commenced. The bulk of the work in post-war days was handled by classes 'B', 'C', & 'E.' Brief details are given here. A full technical description and history of the cars can be found in *The Tramways of Northumberland.*

Class 'A' (Nos. 111-130): Built in 1901 by Hurst, Nelson & Co. (Kilmarnock) as four-wheel double-deck open-top uncanopied cars. Later fitted with balconies & top-deck covers. (All but six sold to Sheffield, 1941)

Class 'B' (Nos. 232-236 & 240-309): Built 1917-26 by Newcastle Corporation Transport. Four-wheel double-deck totally enclosed cars. There were many individual variants in this class, especially as regards trucks and equipment.

Class 'C' (Nos. 29-88): Built in 1902 by Hurst, Nelson. Eight-wheel single-deck cars with semi-open end compartments. Most later rebuilt as totally enclosed.

Class 'E' (Nos. 193-229): Built 1912-1918, some by Brush Electrical Engineering Co. (Loughborough) and some by NCT. Four-wheel double-deck top-covered cars with open balconies.

Class 'F' (Nos. 89-110): Built in 1903 by NCT. Eight-wheel double-deck open-top uncanopied cars. Many rebuilt in various forms later.

Class 'G' (Nos. 170-191): Built in 1903 by NCT. Four-wheel double-deck open-top balcony cars. All rebuilt later to resemble class 'B'.

Class 'H' (Nos. 1-28 & 192): Built 1906-10 by NCT. Four-wheel double-deck top-covered cars with short canopies.

In addition, there were about 10 works' cars and snowploughs in service in 1945.

Above: The driver casts a speculative glance at the photographer as he navigates Gateshead No. 25 along Sandyford Road. It was one of the oddities of the Gateshead cars that they would cheerfully exhort passers-by to 'Shop at Binns' on the front and to 'Shop at the Co-operative Society' on the side. Most transport undertakings tried to avoid such contradictory advice! Notice how the houses had lost their railings for the war-time scrap drive. Very few were replaced after the war, though here they would be inappropriate as car parks replaced the gardens when the houses were converted to offices. *Newcastle Libraries.*

Right: Gateshead 34 accelerates away smartly from the Grainger Street stop with only a few hundred yards to go to the Monument. There is a long queue of passengers waiting for northbound trams outside Timpson's shoe shop. Timpson's is still there today, though the facade has since been improved by the removal of the projecting windows. The shop behind the tram belonged to The Fifty Shilling Tailor, an enterprising concern which would supply a complete man's suit for 50/-, or £2.50! All these shops are surprisingly shallow as they only form a frontage for the Grainger Market, named after its builder and claimed to be the biggest covered market in Europe. It still contains a Marks & Spencer's Bazaar stall, little altered from the turn of the century. *Newcastle Libraries.*

Right: No. 52 and a *Morris 14* saloon pass along the Haymarket, into Percy Street, in 1948, shortly before the tram was transferred to the Gateshead fleet. One of the Class 'C' cars built by Hurst Nelson in 1902, over the years the interior retained its original layout with small compartments at each end. Above the front of the tram the overhead wires can be seen disappearing between the buildings to reach Haymarket Depot. This, together with the shops fronting the road, has now gone. You can still travel by rail from this point, for the photographer is standing adjacent to what is now Haymarket Metro station. *R.R. Clark.*

Above: This was one of seven similar cars built by Brush in 1923 following the commencement of through running and which spent their lives shuttling back and forth between Newcastle and Wrekenton. Like all Brush trams they were exceedingly well constructed and earned their original purchase price many times over. No. 66 is seen here at Barras Bridge, passing one of Newcastle Corporation's 'Blue Bus' fleet. The date is around 1947 and in spite of the winter sunshine it is cold enough for the young lady on the right to be wearing her outsize fur gloves. *Newcastle Libraries.*

Above: A 'last day' picture of Gateshead car No. 71 at the junction of Market and Pilgrim Streets on March 4 1950. Although technically a joint route, the Museum-Heworth service was the truncated remainder of the Chillingham Road circular services and had been worked by Gateshead only since 1948. The following day, Newcastle buses worked in Gateshead for the first time to both Heworth and Wrekenton and the only trams in Newcastle were the Gateshead cars at Central Station. In practice occasional Gateshead trams would work 'extras' to Heworth from High Street even after 'bustitution' and there seems to be no record of the exact date of the last car. *J.H. Meredith.*

Right, upper: Two 'E' class trams, which would have been scrapped many years before if it were not for the economic depression of the 1930s, followed by the War, pass at the Library stop in New Bridge Street. The old Library was opened on September 1 1882, incorporating the books from the Mechanics' Institute. This followed nearly 30 years of argument over whether Newcastle needed a library, and whether or not to demolish the medieval Carliol (or Weavers') Tower to make room for it. It was never a very satisfactory building in spite of its impressive facade and some sections had to be housed elsewhere. It was replaced in 1968 with the current building, a fine design by Sir Basil Spence, the architect of Coventry Cathedral. *Newcastle Libraries.*

Right, lower: An unusual view of Gateshead 42 in Northumberland Street in 1948. This originated as a Sheffield Craven-built tram of 1901, which was sold to Gateshead in 1922. It had rattan seats downstairs and was a notably smooth-riding car. Details of the roof construction, normally out of sight, can be seen clearly. The 'trolley plank' in the centre spreads the load of the trolley and provides a walkway for maintenance. At its centre a casting is bolted, carrying a ball-bearing to allow the trolley to swivel. The pole is a tapering steel tube, hinged at the bottom and kept in contact with the wire by the springs projecting forward. Normally a grooved wheel at the end of the pole ran under the wire to collect the current, but Gateshead used a carbon skid in later years, which reduced both noise and wire wear. *G.S. Hearse.*

Taking pictures inside the High Level Bridge is not easy; its enclosed nature makes a time exposure essential. However, when the bridge was strengthened in 1922 this specially posed view was taken, showing 'B' class No. 235 on a trial trip, accompanied by a police sergeant to control the traffic. The old roadway had been supported by timber beams to carry a maximum load of seven tons; reconstruction work included replacing these in steel. The tracks on this (and later on the Tyne Bridge) were actually owned by Newcastle, although the boundary is in the middle of the river. An interesting point is that the overhead was not wire, but a bronze T-section to reduce noise and maintenance problems. *David Packer Collection.*

Left: Even with the High Level and Swing bridges the River Tyne was a major barrier between Newcastle and Gateshead. The answer was the Tyne Bridge. Like the railway bridges, this was built at a high level both to give adequate clearance for shipping and to avoid the steep 'drop' down the banks at either side. The road is in fact some 93ft above high water and with a 38ft carriageway it can carry four lanes of traffic. The large steel arch form was then very popular and it is no coincidence that the Newcastle, Sunderland, and Sydney Harbour bridges were similar in appearance, the builders learning and improving techniques as each one was built. A double track tramway linked Pilgrim Street with Gateshead High Street and a major recasting of the joint tram services took place after its opening in October 1928. This view shows a Brush-built Gateshead car heading into Newcastle. *G.S. Hearse.*

Most of the trams running on Scotswood Road went as far as the turning circle at Scotswood Bridge, to serve the riverside industrial area. The conductor of No. 285 warns that the car is about to turn into the circle. The straight staircase of the 'B' class car is apparent behind the first saloon window; in front of it is the narrow door. Originally, small metal barriers were fixed in the opening at the trailing end, but the cars were very draughty, especially for the driver, and they were replaced with doors, the narrowness of which caused delay at stops. Completion of this class in 1926 marked the end of new trams in Newcastle, unlike most other cities, which built fleets of new cars in the 1930s. *John Fozard Collection.*

Right: Beyond the Scotswood Road terminus, trams ran for a further three miles through Lemington and Newburn, also Throckley, on the Hexham Road. The line was single track with passing loops. Cars from Throckley on Service 14 ran right through to Heaton, but naturally the frequency was fairly low. This was another route which should have been closed early, but the war gave it a reprieve until June 1946. The original line through Lemington had a steep incline with sharp curves, and small trams worked a shuttle service to Scotswood. In 1922 a stretch of reserved track was opened between the village and the river to eliminate the bends. Its course is now followed by the modern road. Here, a 'B' class tram is seen leaving the reservation at its Throckley end. *North of England Open Air Museum, Beamish.*

Left: Most outer termini in Newcastle were 'stub ends', although sometimes routes were combined in such a way as to avoid reversal. At Scotswood Road, however, there was a turning circle, complete with a wooden shelter and toilets similar to the facilities at Henry Street. This is a 'B' class car. The advantages of the circle were that large numbers of trams could be turned both quickly, and without hindering traffic on the main road. Turning circles are common on the Continent but here only Rotherham and Blackpool operated single-ended trams, and the latest arrivals in the latter town have the traditional layout to obtain maximum operating flexibility. At the time of writing the whole of this area is a huge construction site as the Newcastle Western By-pass is being extended to the Scotswood Bridge. *R.R. Clark.*

Above: Henry Street, Gosforth, was the terminus for both Route 10 to Central Station and the joint route to Low Fell. It was also served by Gosforth Park cars. There was a wooden inspectors' hut, with a staff canteen and toilets, on the site of what is now Hometon House. The buildings at right-angles to the road in the background mark the crossing of the last section of the Coxlodge Wagonway, while until 1930 the Tyneside Tramways tracks came in immediately behind the tram. It was intended that Gateshead trams would continue to reach here after Newcastle introduced trolleybuses but in practice the trams were cut back to Central Station and the entire line was closed in April 1948. The horse-tram depot in Gosforth was about half a mile nearer Newcastle. *R.R. Clark.*

Above: Not long before closure, No. 292 approaches the level crossing with the Kenton & Coxlodge Wagonway just north of Henry Street. The poor state of both the tram tracks and the road surface are all too apparent. The wagonway dated in parts from about 1810, when the Jubilee Colliery was opened and in 1813 a Blenkinsop type rack engine was tried out - the set of wheels and cogs on display at the National Railway Museum are believed to have come from here. Later, the eastward end was closed and the track-bed used for the Tyneside Tramways Company line from Gosforth to Wallsend, but the section here in Gosforth survived the electric trams by a few years. The level crossing keeper's house has gone now, but one stone gatepost survives in Christon Road. *Newcastle Libraries.*

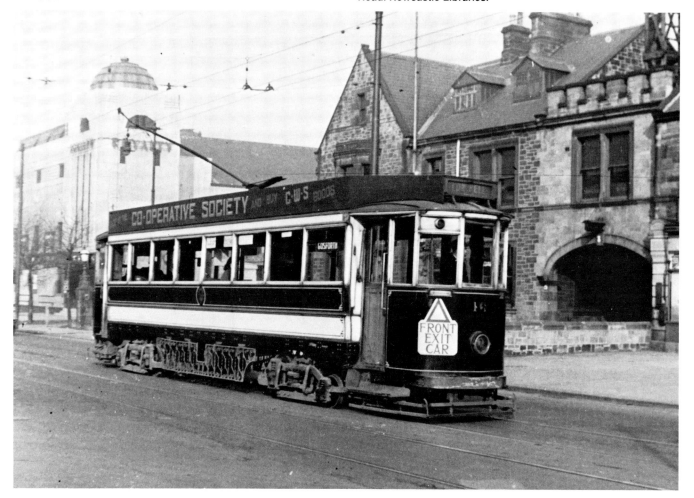

Above: Gateshead car No.16 drifts quietly down Gosforth High Street, past the Fire Station in 1948. Over the arched entrance can be seen the wooden tower which supported the air raid siren. Behind the tram is the Royalty Picture House, now replaced by flats. The photographer was standing on the corner of Salters Road, named after the men from the coastal towns who brought sea-salt inland for sale. In earlier days, Gosforth was known as Bulman Village, after the local landowner. *Newcastle Libraries.*

Right: Not a normal tramway hazard! The conductor of No. 95 is obviously wondering whether or not he is going to be called on to help 'round up' some frisky bullocks in Gosforth Park. The siding for race cars can be seen diverging in the foreground. Gosforth Park was once owned by the Brandling family, but their fortunes declined and the estate changed hands more than once. In 1880, it was bought by the Gosforth Park Company for £66,000. The fine country mansion, built by Paine in the 1750s, was converted to a grandstand and a racecourse laid out. The following year Newcastle Races were transferred here from the Town Moor. Historians regretted the disfigurement of the house, but worse was to follow for the interior was burnt out by suffragettes in 1914, restoration having to wait until 1921 because of the war. The site of the tramway can clearly be seen today stretching away from the Golf Club car park, which is situated on the old sidings.
G. S. Hearse.

Above: On race days, a service of cars operated from Central Station direct to Gosforth Park, special destination boards indicating their role. Just about anything with wheels was pressed into service and one wonders what customers from such cities as Glasgow, where extensive modern fleets were at work, made of relics such as these old 'F' class cars, dating from 1903. The fare was special too, 1/3d single or 2/- return - well above the normal rate! *Newcastle Libraries.*

Below: A sad contrast to the lines of race cars, this view shows the Gosforth Park tramway used as a dump for scrap trams, probably in the early autumn of 1947. The first three cars are the big open-top 'F' class - behind them open-balcony cars stretch right through the wood to the East Gates. In time the line stretched even further in the opposite direction. Already the cars have been stripped of all easily removable metal and they were broken up here in due course. With the closure of the lines leading to the Park scrapping here ended and the last cars met their end at Byker Depot. *R.R. Clark.*

A Class 'E' car, No. 221, heads out of Gosforth Park towards the city in 1947, its balcony passengers no doubt enjoying the late evening sun. From here to Henry Street, Gosforth, the tracks originally belonged to the Tyneside Tramways & Tramroads Company. After considerable argument, through-running with Newcastle trams began in 1904 and the Corporation acquired the track itself in 1930 when the Tyneside Company ceased tramway operation. Before this, however, in 1921 Corporation trams had reached the other side of the Park and in 1924 the link was completed. Known as the Gosforth Park Light Railway, it included a substantial embankment just inside these gates and a cutting beyond the Grandstand. The gateposts, realigned, are now the entrance to the Gosforth Park Hotel and the trackbed can clearly be seen in its grounds. *Newcastle Libraries.*

Below: The route to Forest Hall terminated well outside the Borough. It served a growing area of housing development to the north-east of the city, but as a through route into town had the disadvantage of two railway stations (one on the LNER main line and the other on the 'Tyneside Electric' suburban service) in competition in its last half-mile. Economically, the road joining the two was called Station Road; as can be seen, it was extremely narrow at its southern end and trams turning in from Front Street ran first in the offside gutter and then swung across the road to the nearside. This often confused motorists, like the driver of the Ford 8 seen here. The main line station has gone, the other survives as Benton Metro Station. *R.R. Clark.*

Right: A small file of returning workers strides off briskly, having been brought from town by 'B' class car No. 257. The scene is at the large Benton Estate, built between the wars, and since extended to the open fields on the other side of the road. Although the trams have long since gone, the trackbed is marked by a neat flower-bed in the wide verge of Benton Lane, just north of West Farm Avenue. Trams continuing past here wandered along country lanes through West Moor and Gosforth Park before they joined the busy line up the Great North Road. *R.R. Clark.*

Left: A showery afternoon in Chillingham Road in 1947 as an 'E' class car loads for Heworth. In the background No. 303, a 'B' class, has just discharged its passengers, while another similar car, No. 257 arrives to join the queue. Route numbers were not used after the war, but at one time Newcastle cars on the Heworth route displayed 16 if they were travelling via Jesmond Road and 17 if they were on the southern route through Byker. As the Gateshead company disdained numbers they were probably not especially helpful anyway. Notice the 'Via Shieldfield' board propped on the bumper of No. 225. When new, fittings were provided for hanging these underneath the destination blind box, but later photographs show them in a variety of places - often below the windscreen, sometimes on the bumper, and even one perched precariously on the headlamp! *Newcastle Libraries.*

Above: A superb view, circa 1947, showing Brush-built 'E' class car No. 223 at the top of Heaton Road. It could well be en route for Forest Hall - rather unhelpfully most trams in the North-East only indicated from whence they had come at the rear! Connoisseurs might like to note some of the details of tramcar construction not always apparent, such as the handle on the roof to help fitters climbing aloft to attend to the trolley pole; the metal loop under the bumper for towing a disabled tram, and the delicate way the corner pillars were recessed and highlighted in contrasting paint. *Newcastle Libraries.*

What happened, or even when, are lost in the mists of time, but No. 217 is firmly aground with all four wheels off the rails on Benton Bank. The tram and bus may have had a slight collision. On the left the breakdown tender has arrived. Re-railing a tram was a fairly straightforward matter of dragging it back across the setts to the rails, using metal skid-plates if necessary. No. 217 had seemingly just been re-painted, proving that 'Murphy's Law' also applies to trams. *North of England Open Air Museum, Beamish.*

Right: Whoops! It's August 23 1947 and luckily the unknown photographer had a camera ready when No. 106 became derailed in Pilgrim Street. The front bogie has 'split the points', with each pair of wheels trying to run a different way at the junction. There were 20 of these Class 'F' cars, though over the years many were rebuilt in various ways so by the end hardly any two were alike. The curious position of the controller, actually behind the driver, necessitated the special cranked handle seen here. Even so, the ideal Class 'F' driver was double-jointed, with unequal length arms! A colleague has commented that driving one of these was like having a street of houses following you around! Amazingly, some of the class (including 106) were never fitted with air brakes, relying on the driver's strong right arm for stopping purposes. *Newcastle Libraries.*

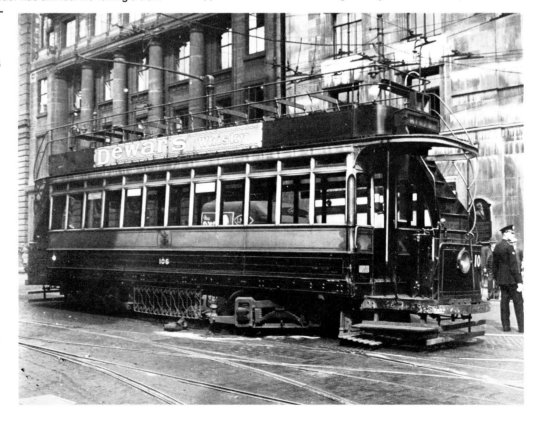

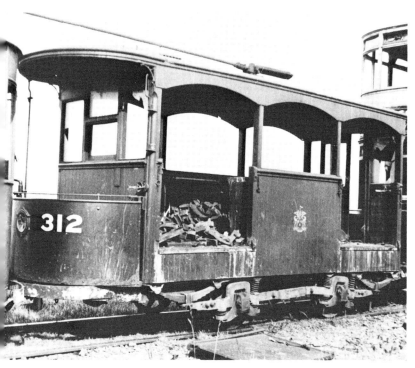

Left: The least-known trams on any system were the works cars. Initially they were specially built but as first generation passenger cars were scrapped most concerns used them as the basis for works cars. Some were barely modified, but the more progressive undertakings built specialised vehicles and this is a Newcastle example, built on an old Brill 21-E truck awaiting scrapping after closure. Bodies were usually simple boxes, as shown here for carrying sand. Others included water tanks for washing the roads, or snowploughs, towing cars, and tower wagons. As road vehicles became more general they tended to take over works duties as they did not interfere with normal services. *North of England Open Air Museum, Beamish.*

Below: Taken long before our period, but typical of workshops right up to the end of the tramway era, this 1904 view shows the paintshop at Byker. No. 107 was one of the 'F' class double-deckers rebuilt from the early open-sided bodies. Behind is one of the Class 'C' single-deckers, possibly visiting for attention after an accident as it was only two years old. This time-exposure was obviously specially posed, the only man in a natural position being the foreman. His 'badge of office' was the heavy watch chain but unusually he is wearing a cap - most foremen in industry wore bowlers. *North of England Open Air Museum, Beamish.*

Chapter 2
GATESHEAD

Not all trams were scrapped when the Gateshead system closed, in 1951. Nineteen were sold to British Railways and moved south to work on the Grimsby & Immingham Light Railway, a curious affair which linked Immingham Docks with the nearby town. Because of this, two cars survive today. Others served as garden sheds and chicken huts! According to Bob Parr's caption, this is one of the 19 cars destined for Immingham, and is seen on April 5 1951. *National Tramway Museum.*

GATESHEAD, the site of the 1990 National Garden Festival, according to Bartholomew's Gazetter, is: "practically a part of Newcastle (with which is is connected by three bridges) and its industries are similar". Like Salford's relationship with Manchester, Gateshead has always felt very much the junior partner in spite of a 20th century population of around 125,000 people. Both towns developed at what was historically the lowest crossing place of the River Tyne. Naturally, this affected the traffic patterns of the area and when the first three tram routes in Gateshead opened in 1883 they terminated between the East and West Stations, on the approach to the famous High

Level Bridge. At that time there was a seven-tons weight limit on the lower (road) deck of the bridge, so passengers from Newcastle had to continue by train, horse bus, or 'Shank's pony.' The first three tramways ran to Heworth, Low Fell and Teams - they were operated by totally enclosed steam tramway engines pulling large trailers. It must have been an impressive sight as these monsters struggled up the steep hills with a full load behind them.

Progress was not to be delayed, however, and on May 8 1901 the official opening of the new electric tramway took place. Like the steam trams in their latter days, the electric trams were owned by the British Electric

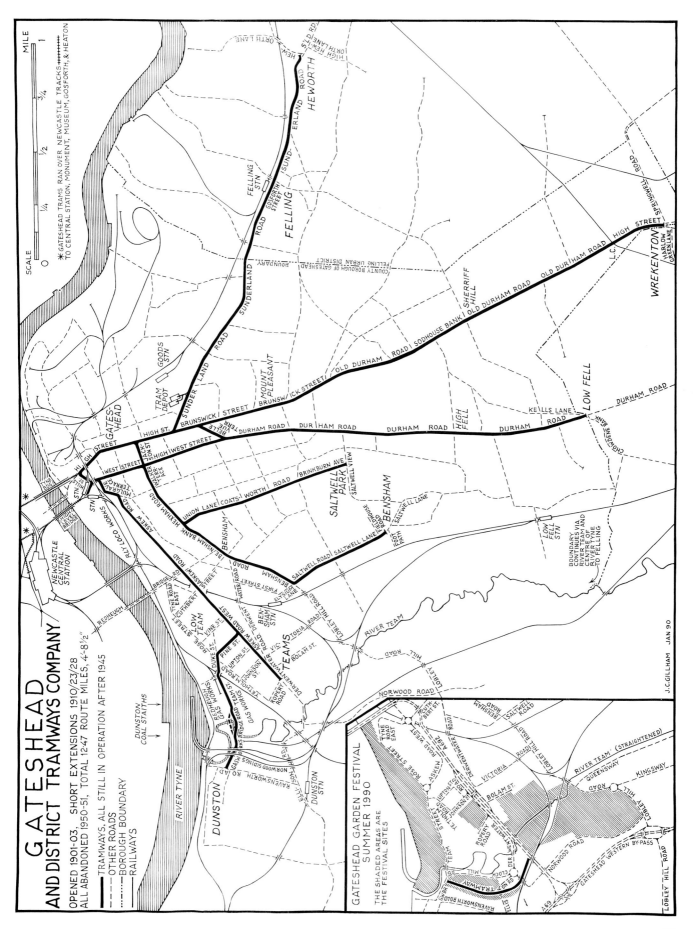

GATESHEAD
AND DISTRICT TRAMWAYS COMPANY

OPENED 1901-03, SHORT EXTENSIONS 1910/23/28
ALL ABANDONED 1950-51, TOTAL 1247 ROUTE MILES, 4'-8½"

—— TRAMWAYS, ALL STILL IN OPERATION AFTER 1945
---- OTHER ROADS
-·-·- BOROUGH BOUNDARY
▨▨▨ RAILWAYS

SCALE

MILE

¼   0   ¼   ½   ¾   1

✳ GATESHEAD TRAMS RAN OVER NEWCASTLE TRACKS +++++++
TO CENTRAL STATION, MONUMENT, MUSEUM, GOSFORTH, & HEATON

HEWORTH

HIGH HEWTH
NORTH LANE

HEWORTH ROAD

FELLING STN

SUNDERLAND STREET
GOSFORTH STREET

FELLING

SUNDERLAND ROAD

COUNTY BOROUGH OF GATESHEAD
FELLING URBAN DISTRICT
BOUNDARY

OLD DURHAM ROAD

SODHOUSE BANK

SHERIFF HILL

OLD DURHAM ROAD

HIGH STREET

WREKENTON
HARLOW
GREENLANE
L.C.

SPRINGWELL ROAD

LOW FELL

DURHAM ROAD

KELLS LANE

CHOWDENE BANK

GOODS STN

TRAM DEPOT

GATES-HEAD

HIGH STREET

BRUNSWICK STREET

MOUNT PLEASANT

SUNDER-LAND ROAD

BRUNSWICK STREET

DURHAM ROAD

DURHAM ROAD

DURHAM ROAD

HIGH FELL

DURHAM ROAD

TYNE BRIDGE STN

WEST STREET

HIGH WEST STREET

JACKSON ST

WALKER TERRACE

BENSWORTH ROAD

BRINKBURN AVE

SALTWELL VIEW

SALTWELL PARK

BENSHAM

SALTWELL LANE

NEWCASTLE CENTRAL STATION

RLY LOCO WORKS

MULGRAVE TERRACE

ASKEW ROAD

UNION LANE   COATS

HEXHAM ROAD

BENSHAM

BENSHAM ROAD

SALTWELL ROAD

SALTWELL LANE   FOLD

FOOT PATH

LOW FELL STN

BOUNDARY CONTINUES VIA RIVER TEAM AND CENTRE OF RIVER TYNE TO FELLING

REDHEUGH

BRIDGE ROAD

ST CUTHBERT

GLADSTONE STREET

VINE STREET

FIRST STREET

BENSHAM STN

COATSWORTH ROAD

LOBLEY HILL ROAD

RIVER TEAM

BRIDGE ROAD EAST

ROSE STREET

DUKE ST

UPTON ST

VICTORIA RD

BOLAM ST

HILL ROAD

DUNSTON COAL STAITHS

RIVER TYNE

REDHEUGH GAS WORKS

GASWORKS BRIDGE ROAD

GAS WORKS

KETHOLM ROAD

REDHEUGH ROAD

DUKE ST

DREWETT

ROPERY ROAD

LOW TEAM

TEAMS

NORWOOD SIDINGS

RAVENSWORTH ROAD

ELL RD

DUNSTON STN

DUNSTON

GATESHEAD GARDEN FESTIVAL
SUMMER 1990

THE SHADED AREAS ARE
THE FESTIVAL SITES

NORWOOD ROAD

TYNE ROAD WEST

A692

ROAD WEST

BENSHAM ROAD

SALTWELL ROAD

LOBLEY HILL ROAD

RIVER TEAM (STRAIGHTENED)

QUEENSWAY

KINGSWAY

ROSE STREET

ASKEW ROAD EAST

DERWENTWATER ROAD

VICTORIA RD

BOLAM ST

ROPERY ROAD

SITE OF No.7 TRAMWAY

RAVENSWORTH ROAD

GATESHEAD WESTERN BY-PASS

A69

LOBLEY HILL ROAD

J.C. GILLHAM   JAN 90

Traction Company through their subsidiary The Gateshead & District Tramways Company. The former company had interests in several British tramways and hoped in due course through their interests in Jarrow and South Shields to build a tramway network linking the whole of South Tyneside. As we shall see, this was not to be. Most company owned tramways closed in the 1930s, Gateshead being the last survivor, but the firm still exists as the publicly quoted BET Industries.

The new electric trams were an immediate success, both with the travelling public and the company shareholders. Other routes were added until at its maximum the system resembled a fan, with the outer terminii (reading clockwise) at Heworth, Wrekenton, Low Fell, Saltwell Park, Bensham, Teams, and Dunston. Services were frequent and cheap - at one time the only fare was 1d! (0.4p). It was small wonder that, on average, each inhabitant made 100 journeys a year on the system.

Various experiments were tried. One which did not survive was for a 'pay as you enter' system, which caused great delays at stops, another was for rear entrance/front exit cars. These lasted to the end, as will be seen from the photographs, and reduced platform accidents considerably. The awkward situation caused by both Newcastle and Gateshead trams running to, but not over, the River Tyne was resolved in 1923, when the High Level Bridge was strengthened and trams ran across it. Soon afterwards, on October 10 1928, the magnificent arched New Tyne Bridge was opened, again with tramway rails across it. Resulting from these links the Gateshead Company and

Right: Whilst most corporation tramways carried the appropriate coat-of-arms on the car sides, the majority of company-owned tramways carried instead a local version of this badge, the symbol of the British Electric Traction Company. Formed in 1896 to develop the new technology of the day, in due course it owned many tram, trolleybus and bus systems at home and overseas, as well as having links with manufacturers and suppliers. Its preferred method of operation was through local companies, which it purchased or created from scratch, and it would be their name which appeared on the 'magnet' formed of bent tram rail. Other 'magnet & wheel' companies in the area included those serving Jarrow and Tynemouth. *John Fozard Collection.*

Newcastle Corporation modified their services with several joint routes across the two towns. Even those routes which were worked exclusively by Gateshead trams continued to Central Station in Newcastle, only workmen's, schools', and various short workings being wholly in Gateshead.

One of the problems with running a company-owned tramway in England was that the local authority was always empowered to purchase compulsorily the tramway, usually at seven-year intervals. For this reason there was no point is spending vast amounts on modernisation. Thus the typical company tramway, apart from some small systems which closed early on, was normally well maintained but somewhat antiquated - the extreme example was Bristol where the original open-top trams ran unaltered until war-time air raids abruptly closed the system. Gateshead District ran into problems of this type before the war, when Newcastle started to convert its tram routes to trolleybuses and Gateshead Corporation considered municipilisation. However, by 1936 the Company had agreed an extended lease with the Corporation and with their approval gained Parliamentry sanction to substitute trolleybuses in the town.

No action on conversion had been taken by the outbreak of war, which of course stopped all such activities. Luckily the tramways suffered virtually no war-time damage, but by 1945 it was, like all systems, rather run down.

In the five years following the war Newcastle's tramways were being converted rapidly and the long joint tram routes ceased to exist. The Company now was not only threatened by municipal takeover, but by nationalisation. And so, although it was even reported that new trolleybuses had been ordered, in 1950 the Company cut through all its problems by seeking, and obtaining powers to operate motorbuses. After that the end was quick. On August 4 1951 the last tram ran from Dunston to the Sunderland Road Depot. The tramway era in Gateshead was over.

Above: How it works. The box on the left is the controller. By moving the handle clockwise the driver gradually increases the current available and the car accelerates. Surplus current is diverted through resistances, which dissipate it as heat, rather like an electric fire. There are normally two running 'notches' on the controller, giving half and full speed which can be used continuously without risk of overheating the resistances. On most controllers (but not this early example) an emergency electric brake could be obtained by moving the handle anti-clockwise past the 'off' position. On the right are the brake controls, the handle operating those on the wheels and the spoked wheel operating track or 'slipper' brakes, which pressed a metal shoe directly onto the running rail. When air brakes were fitted an additional small lever to operate these was provided, but the hand brakes were retained for emergencies and parking. *R.R. Clark.*

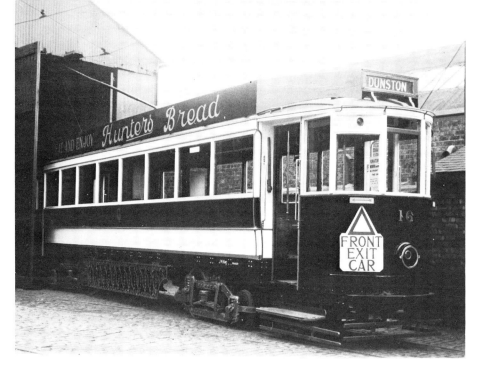

Left: No. 16 looks resplendent as it waits for its moment of glory as Gateshead's last tram, on August 4 1951. Typical of Gateshead's single-deckers, it had two saloons (smoking & non-smoking) divided by partition, and with longtitudinal seating to allow room for standing passengers. During the war all headlamps were shrouded because of the blackout, afterwards Gateshead kept the covers with a small red tail-lamp glass. The forward white lights are visible just below the roof. The bar on the bulkhead folds down to allow the door to be left open in hot weather. It also, cunningly, provides a step for maintenance access to the roof, a grab handle being provided near the rain deflector above the door. Direction indicators were fitted in later years, while the rail over the windscreen prevents the trolley-rope rubbing on the roof edge. *John Fozard Collection.*

Right: An overhead view of No. 48 at Gateshead Station enables us to see that behind the advertisement boards it had a clerestory roof; the small windows under the raised portion could be opened for ventilation. Copied from railway practice and common on early trams, its disadvantages in extra weight and complication meant the feature was rarely used on post-1918 cars. No. 48 was one of five cars built by George F. Milnes of Hadley in 1902 as 'combination' cars, with a semi-open smoking compartment at each end. (A rather similar car, Manchester No. 765, still exists at Manchester's Heaton Park museum tramway.) In 1907, the end compartments were enclosed. The Milnes bogies and other equipment were non-standard and by 1932 all five had been rebuilt with vestibules and running gear similar to the bulk of the fleet. *John Fozard Collection.*

Above: Wellington Street and Gateshead East station, in May 1946. Although the war in Europe was over, its legacy remained: the station name is painted-over as a precaution against paratroopers (or at least those that couldn't read a map!) and the fenders of the trams and the pillar box still carry their white warning paint, used during the blackout. A mixed bag of five Gateshead single-deckers is seen, with Milnes'-built ex-combination car No. 46 nearest the camera following one of the trio Nos. 53-55, recognisable by their 11 windows. *National Tramway Museum*

Above: This magnificent AEC tower wagon, used for repairing the overhead system, was still at work in 1951. It dates from the First World War era and the sheet mudguards suggest it was originally fitted with solid tyres. A splendid vehicle! *John Fozard Collection.*

Contrary to popular belief the slogan 'Shop at Binns - for everything' did not appear on every North Eastern tram - only about 95%! It has an interesting story, which began with William Waples, a draper from the Midlands, joining Binns in 1918 when it comprised just one small shop in Fawcett Street, Sunderland. He became General Manager eventually and remained with the company until he retired in 1964. In 1921 he negotiated a contract with Sunderland Corporation to display 'Shop at Binns' on each end of their trams for £1 per year for each car. In time he negotiated similar contracts with almost every north east transport undertaking, and in other towns where Binns stores were found. The contracts were open-ended and apparently it proved impossible to re-negotiate them until the PTEs were established in the 1970s. Sadly, these trams are awaiting the scrapman at Gateshead's Sunderland Road depot, and include an interesting variety of types. *R.R.Clarke.*

GATESHEAD TRAMCARS

The decision by Gateshead Corporation not to exercise their option to buy out the Gateshead District Tramways Company in 1921 gave the latter an assured 15 years security. They therefore decided to modernise their fleet by rebuilding the best cars and replacing others. This gave a fleet of mixed origins but of three main types which worked throughout the second world war. After the war, to cope with the increasing traffic and the withdrawal of the Newcastle trams on the joint routes other vehicles were bought second-hand. Within the standard patterns there were differences of motors, controllers, and braking systems. A full list with the technical specification and history of each car is given in *The Tramways of Gateshead.* Brief details of the post-war fleet are given below.

Nos. 1-20, 46-50, 53-60: Eight-wheel single-deck totally enclosed cars. Most had eight-window saloons, but Nos. 13 & 15 had ten windows and Nos. 53-55 had eleven. Builders included the Gateshead company, Brush Electrical Engineering Co (Loughborough), and George F. Milnes & Co (Hadley).

Nos. 21-44: Four-wheel double-deck top-covered canopy cars. Three of the bodies came second-hand from Liverpool and eight from Sheffield. The rest were built for Gateshead in 1901 by the Electric Railway & Tramway Carriage Works (Preston).

Nos. 61-67: Four-wheel double-deck totally enclosed cars. All built by Brush in 1923.

Nos. 51 & 52: Four-wheel single-deck totally enclosed cars.

Nos. 35, 68-72: Four-wheel double-deck totally enclosed cars. Bought from Oldham Corporation in 1947. Originally built by English Electric Co (Preston) in 1924-5.

Nos. 73-77: Eight-wheel single-deck totally enclosed cars. Bought from Newcastle in 1948. Originally built by Hurst, Nelson & Co (Kilmarnock) in 1901.

In addition, there were two works' cars, Nos. 45 & 51A. 19 single-deck cars were sold to BR's Grimsby-Immingham line when the system closed.

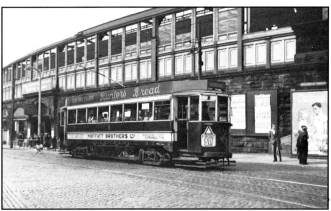

Above: Taking good photographs under the dark recess of Hills Street bridge was not easy, but H.B. Priestley succeeded on this gloriously sunny day in 1939. The track was interlaced to take the trams under the highest part of the arch and the wires were offset, with the result that the trolley head was almost alongside the top deck windows. Low bridges were a recognised source of danger, especially when open-top cars were used. The Bargate in Southampton was especially hazardous and the surviving tram from this system (No. 45) bears large notices warning passengers to remain seated and keep their hands off the live wire! Note the curious 'crossover' in the interlaced track. These points were removed in the late 1940s. *H.B. Priestley.*

Left, lower: The trailing lifeguard 'grounds' as No. 58 turns under Wellington Street Bridge, close to Gateshead East Station. This bridge bedevilled tramway operation as it was too low for double-deckers, although it had been raised four feet in 1948. The Dunston and Teams routes were thus always single deck tram services. The West Street tramway, used by Low Fell and Bensham trams, came in on the right but by the time this picture was taken in the summer of 1951 these had been closed. *John Fozard Collection.*

Left, upper: The heart of Gateshead's tramways was Wellington Street. This was a fairly short thoroughfare, bounded on the north by the High Level Bridge and on the south by the low Wellington Street Bridge. There was an extra exit to the east, under Hills Street Bridge, where the roadway was lowered to accommodate double-deck trams. On both sides there were railway stations raised on arches; Gateshead East (seen here) for the lines East and South; and Gateshead West, serving the Tyne and Team Valley routes. Until 1923, all tram services terminated here, amidst the main road traffic trying to cross the river and it was doubtless with great relief that the company extended its services over the bridge to Newcastle. Here No. 1, a Brush-built car, stands in an unusually quiet street scene. Today, this area is the subject of an improvement scheme and although the trams and station have gone, the little shops in the arches are being refurbished. *R.R. Clark.*

WHEN I started collecting photographs for this book, it soon became apparent that with the exception of Sunderland, the systems concerned closed too early for there to be much likelihood of finding suitable colour photographs. Colour film did not become readily available until the early and mid 1950s and even then it tended to be of low speed and fiendishly expensive to process. However, some diligent detective work by the publishers unearthed the discovery that Ian Davidson

had visited the north east in 1950 and 1951, taking colour slides, using *Dufaycolour* film and I am most grateful to him for making these available to us for this book.

Left: Gateshead car No. 14 waits at Bensham terminus on the last day of service, March 3 1951. One of the basic fleet of eight-wheeled single-deck cars, this tram was built at Gateshead in the early 1920s. The maximum traction trucks, having large inner driving wheels and small outer pony wheels, can clearly be seen. Some cars of this class survived a few years longer on the Grimsby & Immingham electric railway operated by British Railways, but No. 14 was not so lucky. However, two of these cars still exist in preservation; No. 5 is cared for by the National Tramway Museum, Crich, whilst No. 10 works at the North of England Open Air Museum, at Beamish, where it carries visitors from the main entrance to the rebuilt town street scene.

Left, below: The crew of Gateshead car No. 66 pose at Saltwell Park terminus on the last day of service, March 3 1951. The day after, this pair were doubtless crewing a motor bus. This was one of the trams built for Gateshead by the Brush Electrical Engineering Company in 1923, a company which had links with the British Electric Traction Company, owners of the Gateshead company and whose 'magnet and wheel' symbol cam be discerned on the side of the car (see also page 28). Actually, the Brush cars only ran regularly to Saltwell Park in the last year, after Wrekenton had closed. Considering the car was to go for scrap within a few hours, its general condition and spotless turnout reflects great credit on the tramway company and its staff.

Below: In March 1950, Gateshead car No. 36 awaits departure time during the last days of regular service to this terminus at Heworth. This car was one of the oldest in the fleet: it was built by George F. Milnes & Company in 1899, for the city of Sheffield. It acquired a top deck cover whilst in Sheffield and moved to Gateshead in the early 1920s. Even in its last days, with 51 years of hard work behind it, the car still looked smart and only the archaic 'Tudor arch' tops to the lower saloon windows gave away its ancestry to tram experts. Heworth *Metro* station occupies this location today, maintaining the 'light rail' public transport link into Newcastle city centre.

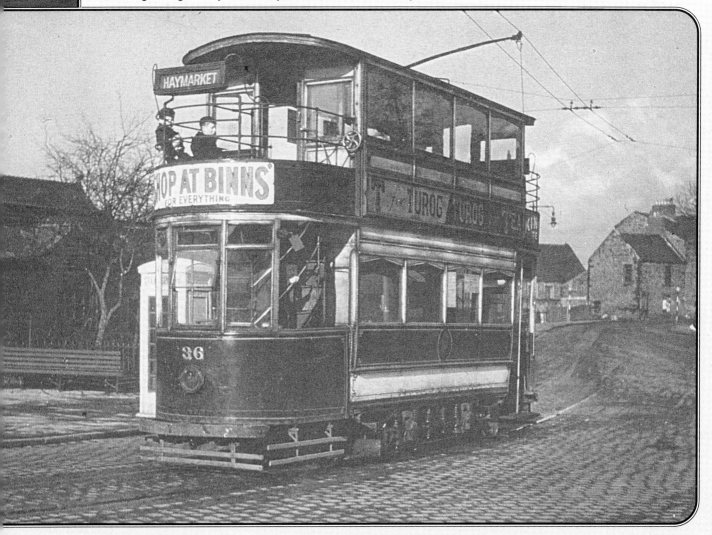

Right: The 'Foot of High Street' reversing point was actually on the viaduct leading to the Tyne Bridge. No. 9 has already swung its trolley and is about to negotiate the crossover in the background. The line under Hill Street bridge came in from the right at this point. In 1950, one passed under the arched bridge in the distance and up the High Street, with its many pubs, but today the arched bridge has been swept away in favour of two unattractive concrete slabs which take the railway over the Gateshead Highway. *R.R. Clark.*

Above: At what is now the centre of the Gateshead highway, two Inspectors are boarding No. 29, as the conductor sorts out a problem with the youngsters on the upper balcony. This car had an interesting history: it was built in 1899 by Liverpool Corporation and after 22 years was sold with two others to Tynemouth & District Tramways, a sister company to the Gateshead organisation. However, they arrived in Gateshead in 1922 where they ran until 1925 in their original open-topped condition; they were then rebuilt in the form shown and survived until 1950. According to George Hearse, they were recognisable until their last day at work by the Liver Birds which decorated their ventilators. *Newcastle Libraries.*

Left: Passengers hurry to catch No. 44 on March 4 1950, the last day that trams ran from Newcastle to Heworth. Years later, light rail transit returned for the whole area on the left (occupied here by the school) is now Heworth Metro Interchange. This terminus moved several times: steam trams ran a few yards past this point to the mill at the end of High Heworth Lane; the first electric trams stopped in the middle of Sunderland Road but the lines were later extended into Heworth Lane, clear of road traffic. In the war, an anti-tank barrier was built across the end of the track, forcing the trams back into the road; with the threat of invasion over, the cars returned to Heworth Lane until closure. *J. H. Meredith.*

Above: No. 9 demonstrates its front exit at Low Fell terminus on March 5 1950. The car is standing on what was effectively Gateshead's last tramway extension - 60 yards of track added during the war to enable cars to stop clear of the Chowdene Bank road junction. Note the lamp on the traction pole, almost certainly provided by the tramway company. *J.H. Meredith.*

Left: A pre-war photograph showing a wealth of fascinating detail on the Great North Road at the junction of The Crescent (Bellevue Terrace) and High West Street. What a contrast to the A1(M), the equivalent road today! The tracks leading right to The Crescent were used in the early days by double-deckers on Low Fell services. They formed the only unrestricted access to the western routes until the Jackson Street line was built, though journeys to Saltwell Park would have been somewhat tortuous! After the joint services began they seem only to have been used regularly by two early morning trips, but doubtless formed a useful diversion, when required. *H.B. Priestley.*

Regular services to Wrekenton ended on March 4 1950, but for a few more months, occasional peak-hour extras used the line. Highlight of the week, though, was Sunday morning and the two timetabled trips. These were ostensibly for church-goers, but in practice seemed to be more patronised by tramway enthusiasts, who revelled in the chance to travel on a 'closed' line. Apparently at least one set of points was removed for re-use, necessitating

'wrong line' working in places. Legend has it that the service came to an abrupt halt during August Bank Holiday, when the overhead gang, tiring of these silly games, disconnected a section of wire and stranded the last tram! However, on Sunday August 6 Tony Wickens was there to photograph what surely must have been one of the very last trips, with No. 80.
Tony Wickens.

Right: On the last day of regular operation (March 4 1950) No. 67 clatters across the Team Colliery Wagonway into Wrekenton. The gable of the Seven Stars public house can just be seen over the sleeper fence. From here the wagonway extended in a U-shape down an incline into the Team Valley. Although the coal depot and winding engine at Wrekenton have gone, the trackbed can still be clearly seen on an embankment crossing the Ravensworth Golf Club. At the north end of the Team Valley the line went to Dunston Staithes and part of the old trackbed carries the Garden Festival tramway. The first part of the line, at the River Tyne end, had been opened as a horse-drawn line in 1669, the last part was to close in 1973. A wagonway museum can be found at Springwell Depot, on the nearby Bowes Railway. *J.H. Meredith.*

Above: Only a few days before the outbreak of war in September 1939, No. 3 turns into Saltwell Road, on the Bensham route. Originally, the double track ran just around the corner, but this was extended up Bensham bank after a runaway accident in 1916. A fine display of advertising decorates the house gable end: products promoted include Capstan cigarettes, Vaux Double Maxim ale and Prince Royal snuff, while the 'bill' at Black's Regal Theatre included Max Miller. *H.B. Priestley.*

Right, upper: Once upon a time, the first two buildings in Coatsworth Road (originally Union Lane at this point) were public houses. This one, the Victoria Inn, which stood on the corner of Romulus Street, has now gone. T. Wilson's window posters are advertising Picture Post, Argosy, Good Taste, Lilliput and Woman magazines, also Gold Flake tobacco and Embassy cigarettes. Old copies of Lilliput are now minor collectors' items; it was a forerunner of today's 'top shelf' magazines, but the luscious ladies featured were confined to half-a-dozen or so black and white photographs, usually making good use of ostrich feathers, to preserve modesty! *National Tramway Museum.*

Right, lower: Bensham is a pleasant residental area overlooking the Team Valley. It was only partly developed when the trams first arrived, mainly to serve the large municipal cemetery at the terminus, but new houses were also built in the inter-war years. Confusingly, the terminus is in Saltwell Road, the Saltwell Park terminus being in Brinkburn Avenue! With these two routes and the Durham Road line, the inhabitants of the large residental area on the high ground behind the town were never more than a few hundred yards from a tram stop. No. 14, seen here, will not be seen here many more times, for this picture was taken in the afternoon of March 3 1951 and the final tram that evening was Bensham's last. Although roof boards are still in place, they carry no advertising - a common sight as contracts ran out. *Tony Wickens.*

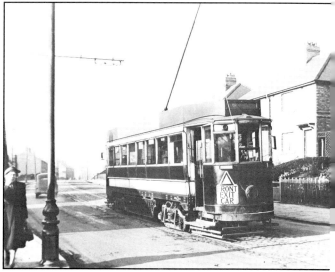

On the last day of services (August 8 1951) an obliging driver stops No. 20 on the curve from Askew Road West into Pine Street, for the photographer. This view emphasises the sharp curves, and the extra 'swing' allowed for the bogies by the use of high floors. Almost everything here has been swept away under the new expressway but amazingly, Horn's building and the next four shops survive! Pine Street is now a lay-by serving these buildings. *National Tramway Museum.*

Right: The Teams route was always something of a lost cause, being formed of the last half-mile of the Askew Street steam tramway left over after the Dunston line was opened. It boasted a tram every 30 minutes to Gateshead Station and was thus the only route which did not cross the river into Newcastle. At certain times it merely ran as a shuttle from Pine Street to the terminus, which must have been an easy, if boring, turn for the crew! The last few yards of the route were actually in Derwentwater Road and like Askew Street this has nearly all disappeared under road improvements. But just at the corner of Derwentwater Road and Ropery Road, standing forlornly beside the recreation ground, there is a little bus shelter. This almost exactly marks the spot where the photographer was standing for this study of No. 55. *R.R. Clark.*

Right: Many of the bigger council-owned tramways had most ornate depot premises, often built in contrasting colours of brick and stone. On the other hand the BET was well aware that ornamentation did not generate profits and Gateshead's car sheds were decidedly functional! Occupying the four roads are (from the left) No. 38 (an ex-Liverpool car), No. 25 (which came from Sheffield in the 1920s), No. 47 (one of the much rebuilt Milnes' cars of 1902) and No. 2 (built on these premises in the 1920s). *David Packer Collection.*

Left: All good things come to an end, but it is still sad to see these well-maintained cars being scrapped after giving a lifetime of faithful service. The contractors are using a small crane and demolishing the trams piece by piece; presumably the enormous bonfires seen elsewhere would have been unwelcome. A couple of staircases lie on the ground while in the background a dump of wheels and axles awaits the furnace. In the early 1950s, scrap metal was still in short supply and there would have been little difficulty in finding a buyer for these parts. *R.R. Clark*

Right: Gateshead depot was in Sunderland Road, with access through the very short Shakespeare Street, where No. 16 is about to enter service. The offices are behind the tram and the tracks curved in front of them to reach the car sheds. The lack of a headlight cover reveals this to be a pre-war view; it was actually taken in August 1939. The Go-Ahead Northern buses are still shedded here, but these buildings are long gone. *H.B. Priestley.*

Chapter 3
≡ SOUTH SHIELDS ≡

SOUTH SHIELDS was, in the 19th century, a rapidly growing town due to its strategic position at the mouth of one of England's major industrial rivers. Naturally, this attracted speculative tramway promoters who as early as 1879 proposed two rival schemes for horse tramways, one of which would have linked South Shields with Gateshead through Jarrow and Hebburn. However, the Borough Corporation decided to build their own tramways, to be worked by a lessee.

By November 1882, the line from South Pier to Tyne Dock was ready for inspection. Alas, the Act of Parliament specified standard, or 4ft-8.5in gauge track, while the Council had ordered 3ft-6in gauge! Opening had to wait until August 1 1883, by which time an amending Act had

been obtained. For three years the six trams (and 37 horses) maintained some sort of service but on April 30 1886 the entire tramway company, lock, stock and tramcars did a 'moonlight flit' - an event unparalled in tramway history! In due course the trams were traced (no doubt by the grooves in the road) to a Jarrow timber yard, but they never returned to the town. Later they were sold to the Isle of Man and, astonishingly, two survive. One, restored in 1989, is now Douglas Corporation No. 18 and works special trips on the Promenade tramway. The other, now No. 14, can be seen on display at Derby Castle Tram Shed.

Although the town was without tramways for a year, a new company took over and on March 28 1887, South

In 1943 when Geoff Baddeley, then a young serviceman, was 'posted' from one end of the country to the other he managed to break his journey at Newcastle for a few hours. In that short time he got as far as South Shields and took this photograph of No. 52 at the junction of King George and Prince Edward roads. This car was unique, being built by Brush in 1935 at the instigation of Mr Fitzpayne, the Manager. Alas, by the time it arrived he had gone on to Scotland where in time he became Manager of the huge Glasgow system and Shields' Council had decided that trolleybuses were the way forward. No 52 was one of the finest trams ever built, with fittings and finish reminiscent of a luxurious long distance coach. *Geoff E. Baddeley .*

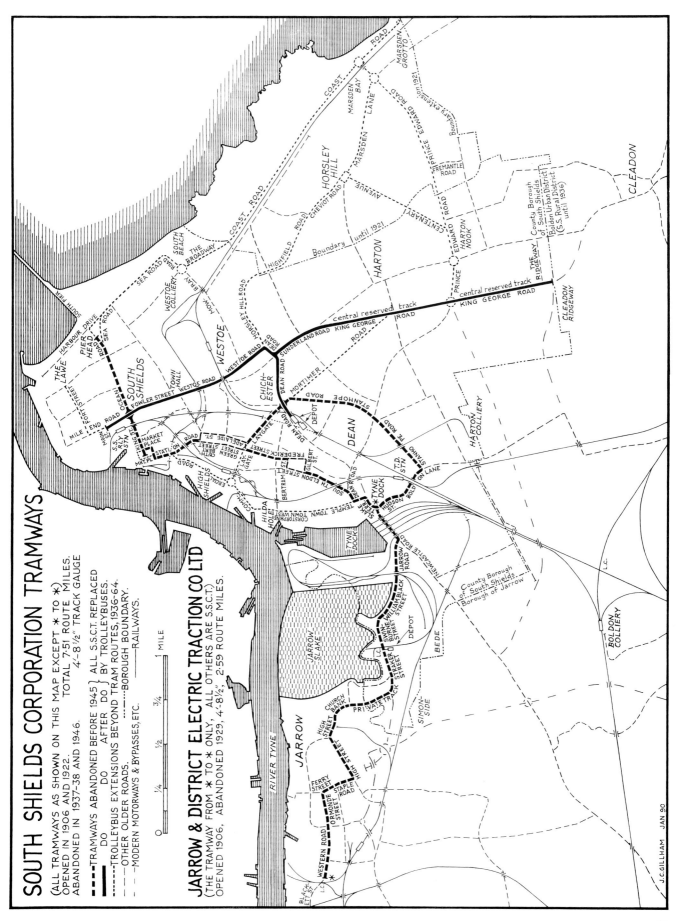

SOUTH SHIELDS CORPORATION TRAMWAYS

(ALL TRAMWAYS AS SHOWN ON THIS MAP EXCEPT ✱ TO ✱)
OPENED IN 1906 AND 1922. TOTAL 7·51 ROUTE MILES.
ABANDONED IN 1937-38 AND 1946. 4'-8½" TRACK GAUGE

▬▬▬ TRAMWAYS ABANDONED BEFORE 1945 } ALL S.S.C.T. REPLACED
▬ ▬ ▬ DO DO AFTER DO } BY TROLLEYBUSES.
┄┄┄┄ TROLLEYBUS EXTENSIONS BEYOND TRAM ROUTES, 1936-64.
─ ─ ─ OTHER OLDER ROADS.
─·─·─ BOROUGH BOUNDARY.
━━━━ RAILWAYS.
═══ MODERN MOTORWAYS & BYPASSES, ETC.

SCALE: 0 ¼ ½ ¾ 1 MILE

JARROW & DISTRICT ELECTRIC TRACTION CO LTD

(THE TRAMWAY FROM ✱ TO ✱ ONLY, ALL OTHERS ARE S.S.C.T.)
OPENED 1906, ABANDONED 1929, 4'-8½", 2·59 ROUTE MILES.

J.C. GILLHAM JAN 90

41

Shields was once again a tramway town. This time the venture was far more successful and operated a maximum of 22 cars but after 19 years the Corporation terminated the lease of the track and on January 31 1906 the town was once more without a tramway.

The reasons this time, however, were far more progressive. From 1896 the Corporation had been considering constructing its own system of electric tramways. In spite of approaches by the British Electric Traction Co., operators of the Gateshead system, they decided to press ahead as soon as they were sure the new technology was reliable and on March 30 1906 the first electric route, this time standard gauge, was opened. Over the next year the rest of the lines were laid, forming a figure of eight pattern round the town.

In this form the tramway continued for the next 16 years, new trams being bought from time to time as the number of passengers grew. A Penny Universal fare was introduced in 1913 and the Corporation also encouraged a tramwaymen's band! In 1914 two battery-electric buses were bought to compete with the various private firms running into South Shields. One pre-1914 purchase was a splendid water car, virtually a large cylindrical tank on a tram underframe, which sprayed a great arc of water to the front and both sides as it travelled along!

At Tyne Dock Shields' tramcars met those of Jarrow. The benefits to the public from through running were immense, but suspicion and acrimony on both sides meant it only happened between 1900 and 1911, and again from 1922 to 1927. The closure of the Jarrow system two years later ended all chances of a South Tyneside tramway network.

Meanwhile, in 1922 the last route extension in South Shields opened. It ran almost due south from the town along Sunderland Road and on reserved track along the central reservation of the new King George Road to Cleadon Ridgeway. Here it was only just over two miles to the northern end of the Sunderland system and many proposals were made to link the two. Regrettably, as with Jarrow, 'parish pump' politics on both sides meant that such a link, however useful it would have been to passengers, was never built.

From 1928, the Corporation commenced a policy of rebuilding older tramcars, both their own and a variety bought second-hand, to bring them up to the highest contemporary standards. The rebuilt cars were given suitable names, probably to emphasise their 'Pullman' character. Names included Nelson, Caer Urfa, Protector, Robert

Below: Once clear of the town, trams to Cleadon ran on a reservation on King George Road, which was attractively laid out with flowers and shrubs. Used extensively in Leeds, Birmingham and Liverpool, reserved tracks gave trams a clear right of way, regardless of other traffic. Properly developed, as in many overseas countries, it provided an off-street rail network much more cheaply than a subway or 'Metro.' This is car No. 49. *North of England Open Air Museum, Beamish.*

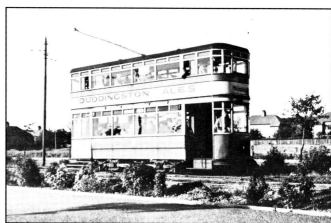

Above: After closure of the town routes in 1938, 12 cars, together with two works cars, were retained to work the remaining line to Cleadon Ridgeway. Presumably the best of the fleet, they included the five 1921 English Electric cars bought for the route, but the rest were a mixed bag; four were second-hand and one third hand. However, they had all been extensively rebuilt at South Shields and were considerably better than many cars in use elsewhere. Unfortunately, closure soon after the war restricted photographic opportunities and it has been necessary to use some pre-war views, though the character of the route changed little in its last eight years. This is No. 51, one of the ex-Wigan English Electric bogie cars ready to depart from the town terminus at Moon Street, shortly before the war. *North of England Open Air Museum, Beamish.*

Ingham and James Cochran Stevenson. Readers might like to work out their connections with Tyneside. The General Manager of the time, J. Austin Baker, seems to have been a gadget enthusiast. He not only invented a device for indicating which stop the tram was approaching but fitted some cars with 'SLOW' and 'STOP' signs, as well as illuminated trafficators for left and right turns at both front and rear. In the event of an emergency stop not only were the signs illuminated but all four trafficators leaped into position and lit - at which juncture, no doubt, the following motorist was so mesmerised he forgot to brake and crashed into the back of the tram! His experimental warning siren (appropriately fitted to No 42, Mauretania), apparently caused widespread alarm and despondency whenever it was used.

Tragically, Mr Baker fell foul of the Tramways Committee of the Corporation and eventually resigned. The town then became far less colourful and the names on the trams disappeared in 1934. A period of severe economy followed, even outdated pre-war tickets being used to save money. In 1935, an Act was obtained allow-ing the Corporation to run trolleybuses, although it was stated that at present the powers would only be used for new extensions and not for tramway replacement. Indeed, one new tram was bought, a centre-entrance four-wheel car similar to those recently purchased by Sunderland - a town to which it would eventually find its way when the system closed.

Trolleybuses started operating in October 1936, replacing motor buses to Freemantle Road. But the writing was on the wall and in May 1937 Stanhope Road was converted to trolleys to save the cost of track replacement. By April 14 1938, all the 'town' routes were replaced leaving only the Ridgeway route with trams. Although it was to be modernised, the war intervened and as soon as possible afterwards, on March 31 1946, the last service tram ran in South Shields.

Thus ended 40 years of electric tramways in the town - few then realised the trolleybuses would have an even shorter life, or that one day the Metro would achieve the long desired link along South Tyneside with Gates-head and Newcastle.

A few days before, on March 31 1946, No. 39 had been South Shields last tram: it now awaits its fate with its fellows in Dean Road depot. No. 52 was sold to Sunderland for £250, the remainder were scrapped. It is possible that 39 could have been the last tram to run on the town routes too, for from January to December 1943 the short Ocean Road branch was returned to tram operation owing to a shortage of trolley-bus tyres. At about the same time, diesel fuel was so scarce that the Manager drafted plans to convert some motor buses to electric traction, with bamboo poles, to save steel! *G.S.Hearse.*

In this 1938 photograph, No. 50, another of the ex-Wigan cars, waits on the short single track at the Ridgeway terminus. Here, as at some other stops, the council provided a neat wooden shelter where passengers could gaze in the direction of Sunderland just over the hill and curse the parochialism of tramway committees who could never agree exactly where to build the connecting line. An extension from here to Fulwell was one proposal, while another favoured idea was to run along the coastal road between Shields and Seaburn. *North of England Open Air Museum, Beamish.*

SOUTH SHIELDS FLEET HISTORY

Most of South Shields' trams were scrapped before the war. The 12 best cars were retained to work the remaining route. These had originated in various places and at various times, but most had been rebuilt in the South Shields' 'house-style', and all were totally enclosed double-deckers.

There were three four-wheel cars, No. 16 (ex-Ayr), No. 39 and No. 52 (the centre-entrance tram). The rest were eight-wheel cars, all built by the English Electric Co. (Preston). Nos. 23, 33, 50 and 51 came second-hand from Wigan in 1931, while Nos. 41 and 45 were built for South Shields in 1921.

A full technical description of both these, and the earlier cars, can be found in *The Tramways of Jarrow & South Shields.*

Chapter 4
SUNDERLAND

Unlike the other three towns in this book, Sunderland is on the River Wear, about seven miles from South Shields. In spite of this proximity to Tyneside it is a completely distinct locality with its own proud tradition of shipbuiding going back hundreds of years.

As the town grew in the late 19th century, to around 100,000 people, it was inevitable it should attract tramway promoters. On April 28 1879, horse trams started running between Roker, on the seafront, to the bridge at Monkwearmouth. By 1894 there were basically three routes, from the Town Centre to Roker, Southwick, and along Hylton Road. Steam trams were tried in 1880 (one of them being a Swiss import!) but they were not succesful and the horses had to keep going until in March 1900, when, after the usual protracted arguments, the Corporation bought the tramway company. Electrification was commenced at once and the official opening took place on August 15, from Roker to Christ Church. By February 1901 the basic routes were complete and the last horses were retired.

Mention should be made at this point of the Sunderland District Electric Tramways. A privately owned concern, this company ran a service from Grangetown by a tortuous 'Z-shaped' route through Houghton-le-Spring to Easington Lane. Opening in 1905, the company was always short of money and even permission to run right into Sunderland in 1921 did not stave off the more direct buses. After closure in 1925, 16 trams were sold to Grimsby and one to Sunderland, which after much re-building became their No. 84.

Like most systems the years up to the Great War were an era of steady improvement with more trams and better track layouts introduced. The war, of course, affected services with over 150 of the staff 'with the colours' and as in many towns 'female conductors' were employed. No. 10 was destroyed outside the Wheatsheaf Depot by a direct hit from a Zeppelin's bomb, unfortunately with some loss of life.

After the war, a front exit layout was tried on a few cars, but it was unpopular and never developed. Ryhope Road was widened, with the tram tracks in the roadway adjoining the central reservation. After some argument with the District company the Durham Road route was extended to the Borough Boundary at what is now Queen Alexandra Road in 1925. Many older trams were rebuilt with the aim of having the entire fleet totally enclosed. In spite of this generally expansionist policy one route was closed, that to the Docks. Traffic had always been light and buses took over in 1928.

All these developments had taken place under the firm leadership of Mr Archibald R. Dayson. Originally Assistant Tramways Engineer, he held the post of General Manager from 1903 until his death in 1928. He was succeeded by Mr Charles Hopkins, who came to Sunderland from Wigan with the reputation of being 'anti-tram.' In fact, until he died in 1948 he was to provide Sunderland with a first class transport system. Within a short time he had reorganised staff and schedules to reduce costs and improve services. He soon instituted a policy of re-

In contrast to the dual carriageway at the outer end of Durham Road (see pages 2-3), the town end of the route had an unusual one-way system. The inward line took the direct route through Vine Place, but outward bound cars diverted from the top of Holmeside through Derwent Street and Mary Street to rejoin the main road. The tracks were laid almost in the left-hand gutter and in places trams passed within a few feet of houses. Car No. 5 was one of eight cars originating with Ilford Corporation and sold by the London Passenger Transport Board in 1938. *Robert F. Mack.*

After the second abandonment of Villette Road, in 1950, a short stretch of line outside the Museum, in Borough Road, was retained as a terminus. It saw intermittent use as routes were progressively closed, and this picture was probably taken in the summer of 1954, when only the Fulwell and Seaburn lines survived. No. 32, one of the ex-Huddersfield cars which took part in the final procesion, is about to reverse over the crossover. The elaborate sign on Shares Furniture shop is worthy of note. *John Fozard Collection.*

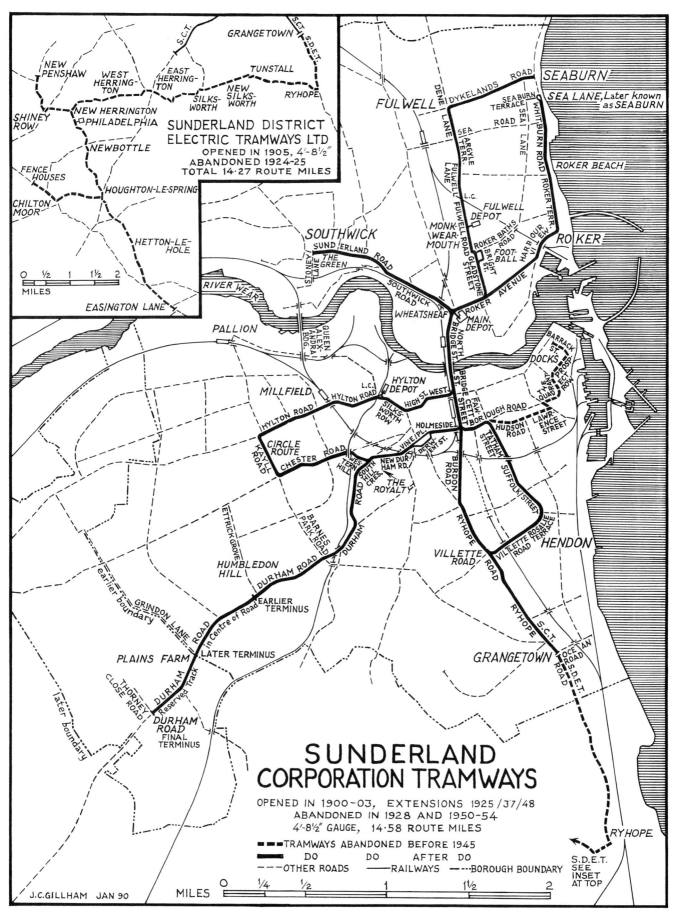

SUNDERLAND DISTRICT ELECTRIC TRAMWAYS LTD
OPENED IN 1905, 4'-8½"
ABANDONED 1924-25
TOTAL 14·27 ROUTE MILES

Inset labels: NEW PENSHAW, SHINEY ROW, WEST HERRINGTON, NEW HERRINGTON, PHILADELPHIA, EAST HERRINGTON, SILKSWORTH, NEW SILKSWORTH, GRANGETOWN, TUNSTALL, RYHOPE, NEWBOTTLE, FENCE HOUSES, CHILTON MOOR, HOUGHTON-LE-SPRING, HETTON-LE-HOLE, EASINGTON LANE, S.C.T., S.D.E.T.

MILES 0 ½ 1 1½ 2

Map labels: SEABURN, SEA LANE, Later known as SEABURN, FULWELL, ROKER BEACH, ROKER, DENE LANE, DYKELANDS ROAD, SEABURN TERRACE, SEA LANE, ARGYLE TERR., ROAD, WHITBURN ROAD, ROKER TERR., ROKER AVENUE, FULWELL ROAD, FULWELL LANE, SEA LANE, L.C., FULWELL DEPOT, ROKER BATHS ROAD, GLADSTONE STREET, BRIGHT ST., MONK-WEAR-MOUTH, FOOTBALL, HARBOUR VIEW, SOUTHWICK, SUNDERLAND ROAD, THE GREEN, STONEY LANE, SOUTHWICK ROAD, WHEATSHEAF, ROKER, MAIN DEPOT, NORTH BRIDGE ST., BRIDGE ST., DOCKS, BARRACK ST., TYNE PROSPECT ROW, QUAYSIDE, PALLION, RIVER WEAR, QUEEN ALEX-ANDRA BDG., MILLFIELD, HYLTON ROAD, L.C., HYLTON DEPOT, HIGH ST. WEST, SILKSWORTH ROW, FAWCETT ST., BOROUGH ROAD, HOLMESIDE, HUDSON ROAD, LAWRENCE STREET, CIRCLE ROUTE, CHESTER ROAD, KAYLL ROAD, HYLTON ROAD, VINE PL., DERWENT ST., NEW DURHAM RD., WEST TERR., SOUTH HILL CRES., ROAD HILL, THE ROYALTY, BURDON ROAD, TATHAM STREET, SUFFOLK STREET, ETTRICK GROVE, BARNES PARK ROAD, HUMBLEDON HILL, DURHAM ROAD, DURHAM, EARLIER TERMINUS, RYHOPE ROAD, VILLETTE ROAD, VILLETTE ROSALIE TERRACE, ROSALIE ROAD, HENDON, GRINDON LANE, DURHAM ROAD, In Centre of Road, earlier boundary, later boundary, PLAINS FARM, LATER TERMINUS, Reserved Track, THORNEY CLOSE ROAD, DURHAM ROAD FINAL TERMINUS, RYHOPE, RYHOPE S.C.T., OCEAN ROAD, S.D.E.T., GRANGETOWN

SUNDERLAND CORPORATION TRAMWAYS
OPENED IN 1900-03, EXTENSIONS 1925/37/48
ABANDONED IN 1928 AND 1950-54
4'-8½" GAUGE, 14·58 ROUTE MILES

━━━ TRAMWAYS ABANDONED BEFORE 1945
        DO   DO   AFTER DO
- - - OTHER ROADS ——— RAILWAYS ━·━ BOROUGH BOUNDARY

S.D.E.T. SEE INSET AT TOP

J.C.GILLHAM JAN 90

MILES 0 ¼ ½ 1 1½ 2

Bridge Street, which carried Fawcett Street to the Wearmouth Bridge, carried a heavy volume of through trafic until recent road improvements. It was this traffic which encouraged the Corporation to link services across the town, but various workings reversed on this crossover, outside St Mary's Catholic Church. This is a notable landmark in Sunderland, dating from 1835 and constructed in stone from Mowbray Park at the other end of Fawcett Street. It was built as a result of the determination of the Rev. P. Kearney, who insisted on a central location. Ignatius Bonomi of Durham (who also designed the town's infirmary) was employed as architect and the building survived wartime bombing to achieve 'listed building' status in 1950. There has been much redevelopment in this area. *R.R. Clark.*

Right: Electricity, like gas, was a municipal enterprise in most large towns, with the tramways often supplying the base load in the early days. In many cases, there would be common management, and these integrated concerns could be very profitable. At least one council displayed adverts on its trams proclaiming how much they had contributed to the rates! Nationalisation ended this partnership but when No. 64, still with a bow collector, passed what is now the Northern Electric showrooms, the tramways and the offices were owned by the people of Sunderland. Note the compressor on the right, with the heavily-rivetted reservoir; it was electrically powered, collecting its current from the overhead supply, via the tall pole. *R.R. Clark.*

Above: On the inward-bound single track through Vine Place No. 8, one of the ex-Ilford cars, passes Soulsby's shop. A bigger concern than this picture would indicate, Soulsby's dealt in ladies' clothing and had a wholesale warehousing side. These buildings have now been replaced, but the shops behind the tram are still there, also the Technical College building beyond. *R.R. Clark.*

Below: The closure of the Circle route was imminent when this picture was taken in late 1953. Early in the New Year this fine tram, just 14 years old, was scrapped and its remains cremated in Roker Yard. Behind No. 52 is the imposing entrance to the Technical College, now Sunderland Polytechnic. Although an enormous roundabout on the inner ring road covers the site of the houses in the background, this point still marks the place where buses on the outward and inward journeys diverge, 26 years after the last tram passed. *R.R. Clark.*

Above: This view of one of the ex-Manchester 'Pilcher' cars on the single track in Derwent Street emphasises its narrow body, a feature of most British trams. The first electric trams were based on the small horse-drawn cars and the clearances on double track routes were designed to suit. When bigger cars were needed it usually proved too costly to modify tracks - only in a few places, like Blackpool, were wider trams found. *R.R. Clark.*

The Fulwell route was extended down Dykelands Road to Seaburn in 1937, coming to rest only yards from the Sea Lane (renamed also Seaburn) terminus of the Roker line.

By the time war broke out again in 1939 Sunderland had a first class modern tram fleet thanks to Mr Hopkins' policies. Yet due to his careful purchasing and rebuilding the cost had been minimal. For enthusiasts it was a paradise, with trams from Accrington, Mansfield, Huddersfield, Portsmouth, and London to be seen at work, as well as the various new cars. This was to stand the town in good stead during the war when maintenance was drastically reduced and those towns which had skimped on renewals before hostilities started found their fleets falling to pieces. No trams were lost completely to enemy action, though both depots were damaged and services were disrupted on occasion. However, the only three bogie cars and the one semi-open car were withdrawn 'for the duration', and in 1944 the long single-decker was sold to Leeds. The sea front tram route beyond Roker was closed for military purposes from the end of 1939 to 1945.

After the war, services returned to normal and the modern South Shields streamlined double-decker was bought, together with six cars from Manchester and one from Bury. The Durham Road route was actually extended in 1948-49, but by then the decision had been made to scrap the trams. Villette Road was the first to go in 1950, followed by Southwick, Grangetown, Circle, Roker & Seaburn. Durham Road went in 1954, part of it being only five years old. Finally on 1st October 1954 a sad procession of nine cars left the Town Hall at 11.20pm to make the last run to Seaburn and back to Wheatsheaf Depot, thus bringing to an end one of Britain's most enterprising and cost-effective tramway systems.

Visiting Sunderland today, one is immediately struck by how small the system was compared with the town as it is now, new housing estates having extended the boundaries considerably. In fact the maximum route mileage was only 13.73 miles, but nevertheless from 1940 to 1949 over 50 million passenger journeys were made every year. Small wonder the undertaking nearly always showed a profit, in fact even the slight losses in the last few years were merely paper transactions in the form of rates, paid by one council department to another.

building older cars to modern standards while at the same time buying such new ones as finances would permit. But what marked him out from most other managers, and, endeared him to enthusiasts from all over the country, was his policy of buying second-hand trams. He was aware that most British trams were basically very similar and as various systems closed he found may bargains, often getting comparatively new cars from scrap prices.

During the 1930s Villette Road was suspended because the single-deck cars used were worn out, reinstated with a high-capacity single-decker built by Brush (No. 85), and finally made suitable for double-deckers by altering the Tatham Street bridge. Bow collectors were substituted for trolley poles and later pantographs replaced the bows — a form of current collection almost universal today but practically never used on British street tramways.

Right: The mid-day sun casts strong shadows across Derwent Street as Nos. 3 and 23 head west to Mary Street. The T-shaped 'Halt' sign warns of oncoming traffic on the Stockton Road, now diverted to avoid this densely developed aresa. The Albion public house on the corner gave its name to several businesses in the area, including the garage on the opposite side of the road. It has since been renamed Chaplin's. The most striking loss in this scene today is the Stockton Road Church spire in the background, which had to give way to the new ring road.
R.R. Clark.

Left: On a sunny day in 1953, No. 55 heads alongside Holmeside towards Fawcett Street. Maynards shop is remembered with affection by many Wearsiders, especially for its wine gums! Nowadays it is Simpson's, the confectioners. The Meccano and Trix advertisements on the top floor (now removed) related to the Central Sports Depot of B. Joseph & Son, which until about 1960 was in Union Street, beyond Waterloo Place, on the right. During the war, they acquired a set of railway carriage wheels - blown out of the adjoining station by a direct hit from a German bomb! In 1943, when the Empress Hotel was demolished by a land-mine, their upper floors had to be removed. Eventually they found a new home next to Maynards at No. 29.
R.R. Clark.

Right: Straggling across High Street West, a long queue of passengers waits to board No. 48 before it sets off to traverse the Circle 'widdershins'. In practice the route had ceased to be 'circular' in 1903, when cars started to run through to Southwick or Roker. However, the cars always bore the 'Circle' destination instead of the more logical Kyall Road or High Street. As late as 1962, an attempt to dispense with the 'Circle' name was unsuccessful due to public protest! No. 48 was the ex-South Shields car and although it was similar to the Sunderland 'streamliners' it had larger cabs to allow for a driver's seat - though apparently this was never allowed to be used in Sunderland. In the years since this picture was taken the new ring road has allowed traffic to be diverted and this area is now pedestrianised. *R.R.Clark.*

Left: Nos. 22 and 71 pass the *Londonderry Hotel* in High Street West in 1953. Nowadays, with redevelopment and road improvements it is one of the few older buildings surviving in this area. Originally the road was called the Sunderland Lonnin, and the *Peacock Inn*, which stood on this site, was the main hostelry of Bishopwearmouth. It was no doubt renamed in honour of the Londonderry family, landowners and proprietors of many collieries in the area. It was by them that the Seaham & Sunderland Railway was built in 1854, parts of which survive on the present Newcastle-Middlesbrough route. The open Morris Minor on the left would now be worth many times its original price, while behind the trams can be seen a Morris Commercial van, a forerunner of the popular Sherpa, Transit, & Trafic vans used for deliveries today. *R.R. Clark.*

An animated scene outside St Mary's Church as No. 92 loads passengers for Fulwell. This picture clearly shows the disadvantages of the traditional centre-of-road position, for all traffic for the Wearmouth Bridge had to pass through the centre of town; such congestion played a major part in the downfall of the British tramcar. The tram is one of the last traditional type built for Sunderland; it is an English electric car of 1933, withdrawn in January 1954, not long after this picture was taken. *R.R. Clark.*

Right: Both the Circle route and tram No. 78 had about three months to survive when this picture was taken in September 1953. The way the town has been built out to the very edge of the steep river banks disguises the fact both the road and railway bridges seen in the background are high enough above the water to allow large ships to sail underneath. The late morning sun picks out the details of the Evening Chronicle's premises across the road. Ornate wooden fittings have been used to convert a relatively plain frontage into a more imposing facade, a not uncommon sight in any ship-building town because the skilled woodworkers in the yards often turned their hands to shopfitting during 'slack' times. Next door is the MoF's Welfare Food Office; its role was to see that children in particular had a healthy diet and I can well remember picking rose hips for the syrup this office issued during the war. *R.R. Clark.*

Until the opening of the Queen Alexandra Bridge in 1909, the Wearmouth bridge was the only road link between the two halves of Sunderland. The original bridge here was built by Robert Burdon, although the design, of cast iron voussir blocks forming arched ribs, was probably worked out by his architect and engineer, Thomas Wilson. It opened in 1796, was strengthened in 1805 and rebuilt by Robert Stephenson in 1858-59. He added wrought iron arches to take most of the load, strengthening it enough to carry both heavy lorrries and trams, in due course.
John Fozard Collection

SUNDERLAND'S TRAM FLEET

Sunderland Corporation operated a greater variety of tramcars than any other British undertaking in the post-war years and to describe them even briefly would fill half this book! When preparing the material I was able to identify more than 20 different 'classes' with numerous variants, among the 91 trams in passenger service in 1949.

Of these, 88 were four-wheel, double-deck, totally enclosed cars. They ranged from much rebuilt veterans of 1901, originating from Dick Kerr and Co. (Preston), to the streamlined centre-entrance cars of the 1930s. The remaining three were the two bogie cars, Nos. 99 and 100,

and No. 61 which was virtually an open-top tram with a tiny saloon to support the pantograph.

Most of the more modern cars had air brakes, as did many of the rebuilds, but there were also plenty of hand-braked cars. Trucks, motors, and controllers were of nearly every possible make and were mixed in bewildering combinations which must have given both the maintenance and stores staff a few grey hairs! Althogether it was a fascinating fleet and those wanting to know all the technical details will find a useful Appendix containing them in *The Tramways of Sunderland*.

Right: A rather poor picture dating from 1950 showing No. 37 (foreground) at Villette Road terminus. This was adjacent to Ryhope Road, seen in the background. This is a view that is remarkably little changed. The house against which the trams are standing is known as Rowlandson House and is now an old peoples' residence, while the building in the background, No. 1, The Cedars, is a nursing home. *R.R. Clark.*

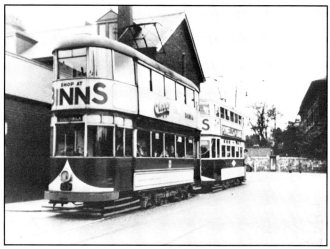

Below: Tatham Street was the 'town' end of the Villette Road route. It was hindered both by a low bridge and this stretch of single track and it was actually closed once, in 1930, when the original single-deck trams were worn-out. It was reinstated with the introduction of a long single-deck bogie car, specially built by Brush and known as the 'covered wagon.' It was so long it was reputed to overhang the pavements on some tight curves! After the bridge was raised in 1932, double deckers were used and the long Brush car sold to Leeds. The roof and parts of the saloon survive in Leeds No. 600 at the National Tramway Museum. The route closed for good on November 5 1950. *National Tramway Museum.*

Right: A narrow stretch of main road near the town centre was Burdon Road, connecting Fawcett Street with Ryhope Road, and taking all traffic heading south. It was bordered by Mowbray Park on the left and West Park on the right. West Park was the scene of some epic football matches amongst local children, with up to 40 players on each side; each paid a penny to play. Nowadays, it is the site of the Civic Centre which replaced the Town Hall in Fawcett Street. This tram is No. 38, one of the ex-Manchester cars. *John Fozard Collection.*

Left: This 1952 view clearly portrays the attractive effect of the layout in Ryhope Road, with trams having almost a reserved track, either side of the central barrier. It also shows the main disadavantage; that passengers could only board in the overtaking lane - a dangerous practice. There were two such stretches in Ryhope Road and one on the Durham Road route. It was never common in this country, but some continental cities used it extensively. *R. R. Clark.*

An unusual feature of the Grangetown route was its terminal siding, sited on the pavement to enable trams to be parked clear of traffic on the busy road to the south. The site is easily traced today and the low wall on the right, reinforced partly by old tram rail, still exists in part. At one time the tracks of the Sunderland District Tramways continued past here to Ryhope and Houghton. There was through running by District Trams from 1921 to 1925 and the Corporation cars ran a workmen's service to Ryhope for about a year. There was some interchange traffic — passengers are waiting for a southbound bus. *John Fozard Collection.*

Right: With work still proceeding and only one side of the new dual carriageway open, No. 96 stands at Grindon Road early in 1948. Ironically, the long-term decision had been taken just over a year before to scrap the tramways, although it was obviously envisaged that the Durham Road route, with its reserved track, would last longer than it did. Plans for the first part of the extension had existed since 1936, when the new housing estate at Plains Farm was started, but had been deferred owing to the war. This set of points was to become part of the crossover in the final layout but oddly no points have been put in the other track. *North of England Open Air Museum, Beamish.*

A few years later, No. 35 stands at the same spot, but in the intervening years the tramway has been extended another half-mile to Thorney Close Road. Today, all the trees have matured and the road makes an attractive approach to the town. On the hill behind can be seen the Prospect Hotel, near the pre-war terminus of the route. It was built, most thoughtfully, in anticipation of the estate and was opened on St Patrick's Day, 1939. Originally it was a Truman's house, but it now wears the Whitbread label. *John Fozard Collection.*

Left, upper: The end seats on the top deck were always the favoured 'perch' of small boys (and tram enthusiasts!) and on No. 93 youthful confidences are being exchanged as the car heads along New Durham Road into the town centre. The bus is crossing the now-closed NER branch from Penshaw, which joined the main line alongside the tramway at Holmeside. This area is vastly changed today with the cutting of the inner ring road; Stockton Road Church is now the site of a large traffic island. *John Fozard Collection.*

Left, lower: No. 8, an ex-Ilford car with its distinctive side windows, is about to pass the Children's Hospital in Durham Road. Traffic following the sign to Newcastle will turn left along Barnes Park Road and thus avoid the town centre, meeting the Circle trams at Kyall Road. The crossover marks the terminus of the route from 1925 until 1929, when the line was extended a little beyond Etterick Grove. Apparently, when the first of these trams arrived in Sunderland it was found to be too slow, so the motors were re-wound to give a better turn of speed. This was successful and a further seven similar cars were bought in 1938. *John Fozard Collection.*

Left: At South Hill Crescent, the Circle trams left the Durham Road route and headed down Western Hill to reach the Chester Road. No. 55 was the first four-wheel centre entrance tram and was built by Brush in 1935 at a cost of £2,400. The same company supplied the steel frames for the similar No. 54, built at Hylton Road. The design owed much to bogie car No. 99, but was 6ft shorter. Even so it seated 60 passengers - more than the capacity of most contemporary double-deck buses. The twin head and tail lights fitted to this and other modern cars in the fleet were unusual in British tramway practice, but no doubt made them much more visible in murky weather. *J.H. Meredith.*

Right: One of the ex-Manchester cars, No. 40, slips down Chester Road, towards the railway bridge at the foot of Western Hill. With closure expected within a few months, road repairs have been limited to 'patching.' This terrace is surprisingly little altered today, although the other side of the street has been redeveloped. Note the ad for 'Vilko Vitalising Kola Drink' outside Bate's shop! *John Fozard Collection.*

Left: The original settlement south of the River Wear was known as Bishopswearmouth and the name is retained in the Kyall Road area by the Cemetery and the Public Library. The Library is in the background, right of the tram, which is of some interest, having been one of the experimental 'front exit" cars of 1921. Unlike Gateshead, the front exit layout proved unpopular in Sunderland, and this car was rebuilt as shown in 1929. As modified it was a success and the 11 others in the class were similarly treated. Presumably the first was the best, however, as it was to outlast all the rest and was not scrapped until after the final closure. *R.R. Clark.*

Above: Unlikely as it may seem, this tram (No. 22) started life in 1901 as a Dick Kerr single-decker, mainly for use on the Villette Road service. When, in 1914, the Transport Department tried welding rails together instead of using fishplates and bolts, No. 22 became a welding car. In 1925, the Durham Road service was extended to Barnes Park and three of the single-deckers were rebuilt as 70-seat enclosed double deck cars with new trucks, motors and controllers. No. 22 was further modified with a Maley & Taunton swing-link truck in 1933. One wonders how much of the original car remained. The corner shop was part of a chain run by William Gregg & Sons of Athenaeum Street; it is now a food shop. *R.R. Clark*

Right: From Kyall Road the northern half of the Circle route reached town by way of Hylton Road. The line skirted the north side of the General Hospital grounds, but most of the forbidding wall on the right has now been replaced by railings and this side of the grounds now houses modern clinics. On the left is the tall stone building of the Havelock Towers Orphanage for Boys, which from 1965 has formed part of the premises of the Deptford and Millfield Community Centre. Both the road service and the rails are distinctly uneven - by 1950 Sunderland had only one skilled pavior (sett layer) and retired workers were asked to return to work. *John Fozard Collection.*

Getting his priorities right, the driver of No. 4 walks back to his tram, tea-can in hand! A *Hillman Minx* and a *Lincoln Zephyr* await a gap in traffic to overtake No. 4. In the background are the Transport Department offices, the *Wheatsheaf Hotel* and the lighthouse which adorned the premises of Messrs Wills. At the turn of the century they were one of the largest wholesale and retail grocers in the area, even importing their own tea and other goods. A fire about 15 years ended plans for the preservation of the lighthouse. *R.R.Clark.*

Left: No. 24 glides down North Bridge Street followed by an Atkinson lorry of the nationalised British Road Services fleet. Beyond the church, is Dundas Street which until 1929 carried a single track to give a rear access into Wheatsheaf Depot. No. 24 was an interesting car. Its basis was one of two Mansfield District Tramways open-balconied bodies bought for £45 each in 1932. This was extensively rebuilt and placed on a new EMB hornless roller bearing truck fitted with air brakes. The odd appearance of these trucks, with the frame arched over the axles, made them instantly recognisable. The sign on Moores Provision Shop does not indicate a 'Rent-a-Sailor' business, but refers to a form of credit once common in seaports. *John Fozard Collection.*

One of the earliest railways (in contrast to wagonways) in the area was the Brandling Junction Railway from Gateshead which included a freight branch to North Dock. It also served trade and industry in the area, one of the last users being Crowder's coal depot, at Roker. Because the line was in a shallow cutting where it crossed Fulwell Road there was a distinct dip in the road, as the photograph clearly shows. The line survived the tramway by about 10 years, but the tunnel at North Dock can still be seen. It's obviously time for new posters and one bill sticker walks ahead with the ladder and paste bucket, while his mate, complete with apron, follows with the rolled-up sheets. *John Fozard Collection.*

Above: No. 61 was unique, a rebuild of a 1902 Dick Kerr open-top car. Officially classed as a 'Turret' car, it was known by one and all as 'the icebox' and except on exceptionally hot days, appeared to be heartily disliked both by crews and passengers. It was stored during the war, but reappeared in 1946, still in pre-war livery and with the word 'Sunderland' still painted out to confuse the enemy! It appeared so rarely it was scarcely ever photographed but luckily it was caught here loading at Roker. *R. R. Clark.*

Above: Car No. 52 is seen outside the Roker Hotel, in 1953. This was Sunderland's last new tram and actually entered service after the outbreak of war, in 1940. Like the three similar 1938 cars, it was constructed at Hylton Road on trucks and body frames supplied by English Electric. The *Roker Hotel*, perched on top of the low cliffs, offers superb views of shipping in the Wear approaches. It has become one of the Grand Metropolitan group Berni Inns, through a series of corporate amalgamations; in the 1950s it was owned by Cameron's brewery, as indicated by the dray outside. *R.R. Clark.*

Left: As the policeman beckons, No. 80 pulls out of Roker Avenue into North Bridge Street. The *Wheatsheaf Hotel* is behind the tram, whilst on the right we can see part of the Transport Offices and the Depot. The island containing the policeman's box is actually built over the tram track connecting the Southwick and Roker routes. This was laid in 1929 for the short-lived Southwick-Sea Lane service. Notice the lady behind the tram lifting the large coach-built pram onto the pavement. Such prams are a rare sight these days, the use of folding 'buggies having replaced them. *R.R. Clark.*

Below: No. 99 was built by the English Electric Company in 1934 and contained many features which were to become standard on cars designed for Sunderland. It was the first to have centre doors and the first to have all seats in pairs on each side of the gangways. Concealed lighting and curved roof lights brightened the passengers' way, while for the first time they could enjoy heaters in the winter. Centre entrances were popular in Sunderland (many of the buses also had them), but only one or two other towns used them in any quantity. Unfortunately the higher price of bogie cars coupled with the extra maintenance and heavier current consumption meant that all subsequent trams built for the town were four-wheelers. *John Fozard Collection.*

Above: One of the more unusual manifestations of municipal pride was the local tram depot. A simple water-proof shed, as at Gateshead, was adequate, but this did not prevent many towns building very ornate depots, usually with lavish use of dark red brick with white or cream terra-cotta. Hytlon Road Depot was one such example, built in the grand manner; it survives today although it has suffered the indignity of a modern extended frontage. It is now a repair workshop for the motor car. *John Fozard Collection.*

Right: The Sunderland Corporation Power Station was behind Hylton Road Depot, coal being brought in by a connection from the Hetton Colliery Railway sidings. This line was worked by a little steeple-cab electric locomotive, built by BTH in 1900. The overhead wire for the loco was connected to the tramway overhead but the rails merely crossed the tram tracks at right angles. Here we see the shunter climbing aboard after stopping road traffic including an Austin lorry with the 'Flying A' badge. One can still see the faded legend 'Lambton Collieries' on the first wagon. The last part of the colliery railway closed in 1972, and there is now a roundabout at this point. *R.R. Clark.*

Chapter 5
PRESERVED TRAMCARS

ONE of the saddest things about the North-eastern tramways systems is that so few trams were preserved. As mentioned elsewhere, facilities for preservation when these systems closed were virtually non-existent. Other systems were closing all over the country, releasing many vehicles well worth keeping, and those trams that survived did so through a mixture of chance and individual enthusiasm. Even so, compared with the large numbers of Glasgow or Sheffield cars preserved, for instance, the Tyne and Wearside areas are very badly represented. On the bright side though is the fact that what have been saved are, in most cases, trams that were unusual in a national sense and yet typical of their home towns. There was nothing elsewhere to rival Newcastle's 'F' class, represented by No. 102, and few other towns operated the long single-deckers so much at home in Gateshead. Many of the types which did disappear for ever were not unique and examples of their type, even if not from North-eastern cities, can be seen at Crich and other museums around the country.

Nothing at all remains from the steam-tram era, but this is not surprising when one considers that about three engines and a couple of trailers make up the national total. Nor have the horse tramways done well, though the North of England Open Air Museum at Beamish does have the remains of one or two bodies that it is hoped to restore eventually. There are, of course, the two horse-cars at Douglas mentioned in the South Shields' chapter, but they were in the town for so short a time they hardly count! With the electric cars the position is a little better. There at present five preserved cars. Four are normally at Crich and one is at Beamish. Four of them are in running order and perhaps one day all five will be. The odd one out is Gateshead No. 5, one of the two little four-wheel single-deckers, which at present is in store without any motors. Gateshead No. 10 in particular is interesting in that, although a preserved car, it still does a full day's work throughout the year as it is the mainstay of the fleet at Beamish. Since the opening of their new Entrance and car park the tramway is used by the majority of visitors to

Above: At more than 40ft long, Sunderland No. 100 is a very large tram; longer than most of today's buses. It started life as a prototype for the Metropolitan Electric Tramways, in London. The 100 production cars were much the same, but with end entrances. After two years as MET No. 331 it became London Transport 2168. It was sold to Sunderland in 1937 and used chiefly on the Durham Road route. When withdrawn in 1951 it was stored until transfer to Crich a decade later. A major overhaul was carried out in time for the Gateshead Garden Festival and on August Bank Holiday 1989 it rolled out of the workshops gleaming in Sunderland red and cream. For the Festival, it has been repainted in the sponsor's British Steel blue; it will revert to its original livery following its return to Crich. *John Fozard Collection.*

Above: Gateshead No. 52 is an attractive little car and was the last survivor of the four-wheel single deck trams often used in the early days of British tramways. It started life as No. 7 and was completely rebuilt in 1920 after running and overturning on Bensham Bank in 1916. As it subsequently received a new 8ft wheelbase truck, it is an interesting speculation as to exactly how much remains from 1901. William Southern, a Gateshead driver, bought it in 1951 and kept the car in his garden until 1960, when shorly before his death, he presented it to the Tramway Museum Society. The motors were removed before sale and it is currently stored under cover, pending restoration. Normally it worked the Teams service, but here we see the car in February 1950 on a Sheriff Hill short working. *Tony Wickens.*

reach the rebuilt town area, which is at the far end of the site, and many hundreds of passengers are carried every day. It is a great tribute to its builders that having had a long working life in Gateshead, plus several more years on the exposed Lincolnshire line from Grimsby to Immingham, it still performs these duties with astonishing reliability.

An interesting consideration is that one day there might be more North-Eastern trams available. One or two bodies do survive and it is not beyond the bounds of possibility that someday they may be given the necessary mechanical parts and returned to service at Beamish. Another idea, which has worked well in the U.S.A., is the building of replica tramcars. Beamish hope to double the length of their line in due course and will obviously need more trams. It would be interesting to see the reaction of, say, Brush or English Electric to receiving an order for three or four trams "similar to those supplied in 1902".

Gateshead No. 5 is here seen at Low Fell, with the conductress about to throw the trolley rope through the open rear window. The picture probably dates from the last days of the system as this car had earlier carried all-over advertisements for Patterson's, the local Ford dealer. No. 5 was built by the Gateshead District Tramways Company at Sunderland Road Depot in 1927. It had longtitudinal seats for 48 passenegers, divided into two saloons for smokers and non-smokers. Originally it had two 25hp motors but after the war more powerful items, probably from South Shields, were fitted. No. 5 was completely overhauled in 1989 and can be seen running at the National Tramway Museum.
David Packer Collection.

This picture illustrates some of the difficulties encountered when moving trams around the country. Nowadays, the Tramway Museum Society uses hauliers experienced in this work. In 1954, however, these were not available and the transport of preserved car No. 102 was entrusted to Pickfords, who towed it from Benton to Bury perched precariously on the small trailer shown. No. 102 became a much-travelled car. After storage at Bolton in the bus depot it went to the Motor Museum at Beaulieu, where it was displayed in the open. It returned to Byker Depot, Newcastle in 1967 and to the Tramway Museum's Clay Cross store in 1970. It arrived at Crich in 1975. Its most recent journey was northwards again to Gateshead for Garden Festival service in 1990. *G.S. Hearse.*

Left: Gateshead No. 10, like No. 5, was one of the 19 trams sold on closure of their home system to British Railways, for the light railway between Grimsby and the docks at Immingham. Ten years later, on closure of this railway, two cars were preserved. BR No. 20 (Ex-Gateshead No. 5) was bought for the National Tramway Museum whilst BR No. 26 (ex-Gateshead No. 10) was retained by the British Transport Commission as a relic. After storage until 1968 it was moved to Consett for restoration, which included fitting some body parts from No. 12. In April 1973, it arrived here at Beamish, to work the North of England Open Air Museum's tramway. It has worked almost continually ever since. Like No. 5 it was built at Gateshead in 1925. *M. Wheele.*

POSTSCRIPT....

Plenty of activity outside the Transport offices on 15th July 1953, with No. 86 changing crews in the middle of the road. This was the 'ghost tram', so called because it was extremely quiet-running, thanks partly to its unusual EMB hornless truck, and because it was built in great secrecy at Hylton Road in 1932. The conductor's box contains his supply of tickets, his waybill, and probably his tea can as well! Outside the offices are parked a Morris Oxford Series 1 and an Austin 10, while the bunting over the door is a reminder of the Coronation a few weeks before. Over the left-hand office window we can faintly read Lloyds Bank Limited - it had moved a couple of doors down the street shortly before. Behind the tram is what looks like a Crossley-bodied Crossley bus on the Villette Road route and almost out of sight on the left is a limousine used as a taxi. *R. R. Clarke.*

Right: When you have finished running trams down a street you have a choice of digging up the rails and hoping that what you can get for them will cover the cost, or burying them under a layer of tarmac where they will remain a confounded nuisance to anyone who wants to dig a hole in the road in future. Often the decision depends on the price of scrap, though if the streets are setted and you want to lay tarmac you may as well dig them up anyway and this is what happened in Sunderland. The operation appears to involve four men, one to work the jack and three to offer advice! In those days the rails were sold and the setts dumped — ironically the setts are now worth far more than the scrap steel. *R. R. Clarke.*